Devotions for
New Mothers

Bonnie J. C. Taylor
Foreword by Colleen Townsend Evans

JUDSON PRESS
PUBLISHERS SINCE 1824
VALLEY FORGE, PA

To the men in my life:
Christopher, Jonathan,
and, most of all, CT

DEVOTIONS FOR NEW MOTHERS

Copyright © 1987
Judson Press, Valley Forge, PA 19482-0851

Unless otherwise indicated, Bible quotations in this volume are from the Revised Standard Version of the Bible, copyrighted 1946, 1952 ©, 1971, 1973 by the Division of Christian Education of the National Council of the Churches of Christ in the U.S.A., and used by permission.

Other versions of the Bible quoted in this book are:
The New English Bible (NEB). Copyright © The Delegates of the Oxford University Press and the Syndics of the Cambridge University Press 1961, 1970.
The *Good News Bible*, the Bible in Today's English Version. Copyright © American Bible Society, 1976. Used by permission.
HOLY BIBLE New International Version, copyright © 1978, New York International Bible Society. Used by permission.
The Living Bible. Tyndale House Publishers, Wheaton, Ill. Used by permission.
The Holy Bible, King James Version.
The *New American Standard Bible*, © The Lockman Foundation 1960, 1962, 1963, 1968, 1971, 1972, 1973, 1975, used by permission.
The Jerusalem Bible, copyright © 1966 by Darton, Longman, and Todd, Ltd., and Doubleday and Company, Inc. Used by permission of the publisher.

Library of the Congress Cataloging-in-Publication Data

Taylor, Bonnie J. C.
    Devotions for new mothers.

    1. Mothers—Prayer-books and devotions—English.
I. Title.
BV4847.T35   1987   242'.6431   86-27380
ISBN 0-8170-1081-5
ISBN 0-8170-1115-3 (pbk.)

Printed in the U.S.A.
Fifth printing, 2010

To _____

From _____

_____
Date

Contents

Section 3: Seeking God's Guidance ... 83

Foreword

M any years ago when our first child was born, someone who had come to visit me in the hospital left a slim, paperbound book by my bed. While I have forgotten who the "someone" was or who authored that collection of devotions, I remember well the impact that little book had on me. Lying in bed in that high ceilinged room in Edinburgh's Simpson Maternity Pavillion, I read its pages again and again—and wept without the slightest tinge of embarrassment or shame.

Is a woman *ever* more vulnerable or more open to the work of God in her life than when she has just experienced the miracle of birth? If there is such a time, I am not aware of it. Birthing a child ushered me into a new arena where I experienced joys—and fears—I had never known before. I felt I was living at the very edge of my emotions, and that simple little volume by my bed helped me yield those new, tender feelings to the God of all creation. It also gave me assurance that as my husband, Louie, and I took on the awesome responsibility of parenting, we would not walk alone.

No wonder, then, that in the years that followed I often wished I had a supply of those books to pass on to other new mothers. But, alas, it seemed to have disappeared from the bookstores of the world as mysteriously as it had first entered my life.

Imagine my delight to discover, after all this time, that such a book has been written—and, in my opinion, very well written indeed!

Bonnie Taylor's *Devotions for New Mothers* is wonderful! It is warm, honest, and very human. As you read it, you will laugh, cry, and—if you are like me—recognize yourself on almost every page. What is more important, your thoughts will be centered on Christ as the one who not only *blesses* us in motherhood but continually and lovingly works in us to make us more than we are—and all he means us to be.

The fact that Bonnie and C.T. are special people in the life of my family makes recommending her book a very personal pleasure for me. However, what I say here stands independent of our friendship. This is a book that needed to be written. I commend it to you. I invite you to share the joy of these *Devotions for New Mothers* with me.

Colleen Townsend Evans
Washington, D.C.
September 1986

Introduction

*I*t was a bright and sunny New England afternoon on Cape
Cod when this book began to take shape. My son Christopher and I had flown to the Cape a week ahead of my husband, CT, to spend some time with family and allow me to get some rest. Little did I know that just because I left my responsibilities at home did not mean that my three-month-old son would allow me a vacation!

I was lonely and tired and taken by surprise at the feelings churning within me. *What kind of a mother am I,* I wondered, *to experience so many conflicting feelings all at once?* I hadn't felt this confused since I was an adolescent!

As I searched the bookstores, I found little comfort. Most of the books I saw dealt with this initial encounter with motherhood as merely a fleeting stage—one that both my child and I would soon outgrow. Although I knew that there was some real truth in this, that knowledge didn't help this phase pass any more quickly or enable me to deal with the emotions and adjustments I was being faced with any better. I needed to know that someone else understood the joys as well as the trials these long days held. I needed to know that I wasn't alone.

When CT arrived at the Cape for our family vacation, I shared with him my frustration at not finding a resource to help me handle not just the joys but some of the difficult times that motherhood brings with it. He suggested that this might be God's call to step out in faith and speak to this special need.

As I strained to hear God's voice and seek his guidance to lead me through the maze of new responsibilities, his Spirit met me on every foot of new ground. If, as you read the devotions which follow, from time to time you find yourself saying, "I relate to that—I know just how she felt," then this book has accomplished its mission.

This book was not meant to be read in one sitting. It was written with the hope that you might place it on your night stand, in the nursery next to a rocking chair, or any place else where you might find a few minutes in the midst of a busy day to dip in. I hope you find comfort, hope, and a few laughs between its covers.

I have many, many thanks to express. The completion of this project is truly a miracle in which countless people had a part. First, thank you to the many women who were willing to share their stories, that God might use their experience to bring guidance and comfort to others. The names and dates have been changed, and some of the characters presented in the devotions are compilations of several women who voiced similar feelings when faced with similar situations. Next, thank you to both of my families, the Calligans and the Taylors, who expressed their support in uncounted ways. Mom, I especially want to express my appreciation to you. Without your example of stamina during very tough times and the availability of your unconditional love and support, I never would have attempted something which seemed so very much out of my league.

Two people who deserve special notes of appreciation are my long-time good friend, Jerry Graham, and my beloved husband, CT. Thank you, Jerry, for not only seeing God's hand at work in my life but also for caring enough to share your insight with me. By holding me accountable, you helped me be a better steward of God's gracious gifts.

Last, but certainly not least, I owe my deepest appreciation to my husband. CT, you are the one person whom God used most to poke, prod, and otherwise motivate me to accomplish this work. Thanks for believing in me and acting as God's instrument to polish this "diamond in the rough."

Bringing Baby Home

When a woman is in travail she has sorrow, because her time has come; but when she is delivered of the child, she no longer remembers the anguish, for joy that a child is born into the world.

John 16:21

Birth: the Anguish and the Joy

John 16:21. "When a woman is in travail she has sorrow, because her hour has come; but when she is delivered of the child, she no longer remembers the anguish, for joy that a child is born into the world."

---

*I*t's a boy! A beautiful, bald, healthy boy! We were convinced he was going to be a girl and awaited her arrival with great joy. Although surprised, we are just as delighted to receive a son.

It has only been hours since his birth, but I know those unforgettable moments of our first encounter will remain in my heart forever:

The fear and anxiety of labor which overshadowed the last months of my pregnancy were behind me. I had endured both the early and active phases of labor and gone through transition. We were coming down the home stretch. The doctor examined me and said, "This is it. It's up to you, Bonnie. We can be here for hours or only a matter of minutes. Let's make every contraction really pay. Push now, for all you're worth!" I used every ounce of energy I had left to concentrate on the delivery of my child. Soon the head crowned, and the doctor exclaimed, "He or she is a real baldy!" Forty-five minutes later, Christopher Calligan Taylor was born.

As the doctor placed our wailing son on my abdomen, the nurse positioned a heat lamp over the three of us—our son, my husband, and me—to protect Ohio's newest resident from the

cold. While Christopher's voice filled the room, his daddy—
CT—and I shared a moment of speechless joy as we listened
with awe to that cry which would forever change our lives.

It is now well past midnight. Our families and friends have
been called, CT has gone home for a much deserved night's
rest, but my adrenalin is still pumping. I know that sleep is
hours away for me.

I am experiencing many emotions. As I watch Christopher
sleep in his bassinet next to my bed, I am so thankful that God
has blessed us with a healthy child and a safe delivery. I am
struck by the depth of closeness CT and I felt as we experienced
the bittersweet process of giving birth. And I am scared and a
little overwhelmed by the responsibility that lies ahead. Lord,
please enable me to be a good mother.

PRAYER: Dear Lord, thank you for the new life You have
shared with us this day. Thank you for deepening Your gifts of
love and joy in our family through the birth of a precious new
soul. Amen.

A Lifetime to Nurture

2 Timothy 1:5. I am reminded of the sincerity of your faith, a faith which was alive in Lois your grandmother and Eunice your mother before you, and which, I am confident, lives in you also (NEB).

With great excitement Tracy felt her labor begin on a Friday afternoon in late December. Mild and irregular at first, her contractions did not pick up until the next morning. By 7 P.M. Saturday evening they had intensified to the point where she was admitted to the hospital. Expecting an uncomplicated vaginal delivery, the nurses helped her and her husband Greg settle into a birthing room. Although she knew the next few hours would be trying, she tingled with excitement as she anticipated the joy of cradling her newborn child in her arms.

By Sunday morning it was apparent that something was wrong. The contractions were steady, but they weren't strong enough to make any progress. At 4 P.M. the doctor moved Tracy from the birthing room to a labor room where they could administer pitocin to strengthen and quicken her contractions. After four long hours of hard and constant labor, it was discovered that the baby's position would not allow it to progress down the birth canal. At that point the doctor decided to perform a cesarean section.

Tracy fell into a deep sleep after the surgery was performed. Hours later she awoke to the hammering of a splitting headache and an overwhelming feeling of despair. She felt that she had let everyone down: herself, her husband, her family, even God. She had envisioned a "natural birth" where she and Greg would share the delivery with as little assistance from the doctor as possible. Then, within moments the child would be placed on her stomach as it experienced its first encounter with the world outside the protective womb. But that wasn't the way it turned out. For some reason the doctor didn't bring her daughter to her immediately but waited until she was clean and wrapped in a blanket. Then Tracy couldn't hold her. Both arms were restrained: one with an IV, the other with a blood-pressure cuff and other monitors. And as if she hadn't experienced enough disappointment, soon after her little girl arrived, Tracy became nauseated by the anesthetic. This wasn't the experience she had prepared for, and it seemed too much to bear.

Tracy's recuperation kept her in the hospital for a week. At first she felt lost in despair, feeling that her body had been useless, giving her child something less than the best. But as the days passed the Holy Spirit seemed to be whispering words of comfort in her ear. One Scripture in particular inspired new hope in her. It was 2 Timothy 1:5, which speaks of the importance of a mother's faith and the influence it has upon her children. As Tracy meditated upon the passage, she realized that although her body may have had difficulty bringing this new life into the world, it would be her faith that would nurture and sustain this little girl through all the years to come. Her excitement was rekindled as she saw a new and great challenge set before her: the lifetime task of communicating God's love to this child.

PRAYER: Dear God, thank you for the way Your Holy Spirit moves to inspire new hope in our hearts just at the point when we feel the most defeated. Thank you also for flooding our lives with such a great and holy purpose. Amen.

Letting Love Mature

2 Corinthians 12:9a. "My grace is sufficient for you, for my power is made perfect in weakness."

*K*aren gave birth to her first child in the dead of winter at a northern Ohio hospital. As her seven-pound son slept in his bassinet next to her bed, she watched the snow fall outside her window through the blur of tear-filled eyes.

"How do you feel today, Karen?" Her preoccupation allowed the doctor to enter the room unnoticed.

Karen, firmly in the grips of postpartum blues, hesitated. As the tears spilled down her cheeks, she slowly replied, "I'm afraid I don't love my baby the way he needs to be loved."

The doctor, hearing the fear in her trembling voice and sensing her desire to do what was best for her child, gently asked, "How long did it take you to discover your love for your husband when the two of you first met?"

Thinking a moment, she replied, "Why, quite a while."

"Well," said the doctor, "it might take you a while to discover the depth of the love you have for this new person as well."

As Karen reflected upon the insightful doctor's statement, she began to realize the presence of God's grace at work in her life. Because of that grace, she would be able to nurture and care for her son while the seeds of love for her child matured.

PRAYER: Lord, thank you for the presence of Your power and grace when we feel inadequate to the task of providing for all the needs of a growing child. Amen.

Bound for Home

John 3:3. Jesus answered, "I am telling you the truth: no one can see the Kingdom of God unless he is born again" (TEV).

*L*iberation Day! The doctor appeared in my room at 7 A.M., examined me, and said that if I was careful and took it easy, I could be released. What wonderful news, for I longed to be in my own home!

While the nurse took Christopher to the nursery for his bath, I called CT and gave him the good news. Then I hopped in the shower and primped until my little one was returned to my room. I wanted both of us to be as beautiful as possible for our homecoming.

Upon Christopher's return, I pulled out the layette CT had brought the night before—white stretchy pj's and a white crocheted sweater sent by his grandmother. He looked like a little angel. Dad arrived, we signed the necessary forms, and we were off.

The brilliance of a beautiful May morning. embraced us as we stepped out of the hospital doors. The whole world sparkled with a new freshness. When we arrived home and settled in, it was as if I'd never been there before. The furnishings were familiar, but now I saw God's gentle touch everywhere. The warmth of his presence assured me that our home was nestled deep within the protective palm of our Father, God.

God had opened my eyes to a whole new dimension of life through the birth of our son. Old and familiar things were renewed with the purpose of providing for this young life. To him all was new, as if created afresh at his seeing. It caused me to remember my experience of being born anew in the Spirit. Christ's redemptive, loving power, although unknown to me, had accompanied me throughout my life. Then one day, by the rebirth of my spirit, my eyes were opened, and I saw Christ as he truly is: my compassionate Savior and Lord.

PRAYER: Thank you, Lord, for the opportunity of new insight which you provide through these tiny new people in our lives. Keep us open so that we might continue to receive Your word from their fresh perspective. Amen.

Being Vulnerable

Read Luke 1:26–56.

Luke 1:46–49.

And Mary said,
  "My soul magnifies the Lord,
  and my spirit rejoices in God my Savior,
  for he has regarded the low estate of his handmaiden.
  For behold, henceforth all generations will call me blessed;
  for he who is mighty has done great things for me,
  and holy is his name."

Mary's heart soared, for another mortal knew her secret. Her cousin Elizabeth, enlightened by the Holy Spirit, acknowledged the holy child harbored safely within Mary's womb. "Blessed are you among women, and blessed is the fruit of your womb!" she exclaimed as the child within her own body leaped at the sound of Mary's voice.

Mary now had someone with whom she could share her innermost feelings. Elizabeth, being six months pregnant herself by divine intervention, understood that with God nothing is impossible. She was the friend Mary desperately needed at this awesome and bewildering time in her life. Who else would have believed her? Who else could truly share her joy? Because of Elizabeth's love and acceptance, Mary was freed to share the emotions she felt at the revelation of her expected son. What beautiful praise she expressed to her Lord and Savior! How humble she felt in light of the magnitude of the blessing God had bestowed upon her! She would be the mother of the Messiah!

How difficult it must have been for Mary to keep her emotions bottled up inside! But our gracious God provided for her—sending her to the one person who could really listen to and understand Mary's feelings.

As mothers, we experience new and unexpected demands daily. It is easy to feel as though no one has walked this path before. But God places us in a body of believers. Our brothers and sisters in Christ are God's listening ears and loving arms in our lives. We must take a chance and share that tender part of our being which we jealously guard. For when we can do that, we discover that through others Jesus himself is binding our wounds, expanding our dreams, and celebrating our joys.

PRAYER: Dear Lord, send to each of us a friend like Elizabeth—one who possesses the spiritual sensitivity to help unlock our feelings so that we might more fully experience Your presence. Amen.

Elusive Moments of Peace

Isaiah 41:10

> Fear not, for I am with you,
>   be not dismayed, for I am your God;
> I will strengthen you, I will help you,
>   I will uphold you with my victorious
>   right hand.

*B*onnie, are you awake?" CT whispered as he shook me gently.

"I am now," I groaned.

"I think Christopher is hungry again."

"He can't be; I just fed him!"

"I've tried everything and I can't get him to stop crying. Do you think you could try feeding him?"

"I suppose," I snapped as I pulled myself up off the couch.

Why can't I have just one hour of peace, I thought as I trudged up the stairs to the nursery.

I was having a tough time adjusting to breast feeding. In keeping with the pediatrician's advice, I was feeding Christopher on demand. But his demands and my biological clock were not in sync, especially at night! It seemed as though every time I would drift off to sleep, his stomach would wake up. Then, having been awakened, it would take me quite awhile to settle down once more. But that was never the end of it, for just as sleep arrived—you guessed it—he would cry for more food.

It's a wonderful feeling to provide sustenance for another

human being from my own body. The closeness is unlike any other experience in life. But as satisfying an experience as it is, I still find it to be draining. It drains my strength—physical, mental, and emotional. My body is no longer mine alone. I not only share it with my husband, but now, while I am breast feeding, I have a child who needs it as well. The lack of privacy can be tiring, frustrating, and at times seem downright unfair.

I am really counting on the power of the Holy Spirit to enable me to respond appropriately to my child with each new circumstance which presents itself. Christopher and I have only begun our pilgrimage as parent and child, and already I am faced with my inadequacies. I am thankful that the God of all the universe has promised to strengthen, help, and uphold me as I walk in his paths.

PRAYER: Thank you, Lord, that You are not a God who hands us a responsibility and then steps back to watch how we deal with it. You are present, moment by moment, helping, strengthening, and enabling your children to carry out the charge You place before us. Teach us never to hesitate to call on You for help and guidance. Amen.

Wounding and Being Forgiven

Philippians 2:13. For God is at work in you, both to will and to work for his good pleasure.

I yelled at my mother today. She traveled almost three thousand miles just to be by my side and help care for her new grandson, and I yelled at her! As the words tumbled out of my mouth, I wanted to push them right back inside, but it was too late.

I was feeling tired and cranky. My stitches were pulling from getting up and down too much, and we were expecting yet another batch of company. She made a comment that, coming from anyone else, would have been received with the purpose intended—one of consolation. But since the statement came from my *mother*, it pushed my anger and pride buttons instead. For a moment it was as if I were sixteen again, declaring my independence and trying to prove that I was an adult. As I snapped at her, her eyes revealed the hurt she felt, and I felt awful.

Why is it that the same advice which is welcomed from friends and even strangers is perceived as meddling when it comes from our parents? I apologized immediately, but it was too late. A lethal emotional blow had been struck, for no one knows each other's weaknesses as well as mothers and daughters do.

I have been greatly blessed with a mother who loves me unconditionally. While the hurt still lingered in her eyes, she extended her arms in forgiveness. She would not allow the residue of one painful moment to taint the rest of her stay with us.

I am especially thankful that God is at work in me when my darker side rears its ugly head. His grace and power washed away the walls of pride and selfishness that would have kept me from receiving that badly needed forgiveness. By his Holy Spirit, he enabled us both to desire and accomplish his loving purpose of reconciliation.

PRAYER: Thank you, Father, that You reign supreme in our lives even when we feel overpowered by our own sinfulness. Your healing forgiveness reaches out to bind not only our wounds but also the wounds our sinful actions inflict on others. Help us to work with You to accomplish Your good pleasure and not our own selfish desires. Amen.

When Baby Returns
to the Hospital

1 Corinthians 10:13. And God is faithful; he will not let you be tempted beyond what you can bear. But when you are tempted, he will also provide a way out so that you can stand up under it (NIV).

K ate had a long and arduous delivery, but, finally, on a wintry Sunday afternoon, she gave birth to a small but seemingly strong and robust little girl.

The first week went fairly smoothly—in spite of a slightly prolonged stay at the hospital when Dana developed jaundice. But toward the end of that week Kate felt a growing uneasiness. Dana was sleeping more and more and nursing less and less. By Monday afternoon, just eight days after Dana's birth, Kate knew there was something seriously wrong with her child.

Kate and her husband, John, bundled Dana up and took her to see the doctor. From there they were sent directly to the hospital for some more tests, and at midnight Dana was readmitted.

The doctors insisted that Kate go home. It was too soon after Dana's birth for her to be holding an all-night vigil. She needed her rest; her body needed to continue its recovery. Besides, the doctors argued, she wouldn't be permitted to hold her daughter anyway because Dana had to remain under the special lights designed to help eradicate the jaundice.

At the same time that they were insisting that Kate go home, the doctors also decided that they would take Dana off her mother's milk. They suspected that she might have an intolerance to it.

As things turned out, their suspicions were well founded. Dana could not digest Kate's milk—partly because the milk was too rich and partly because she was so small that her digestive tract had not developed enough to digest it. Once the real problem was diagnosed, Kate felt both useless and relieved—useless in that she couldn't do anything to help, but relieved that her little girl was eventually going to be all right and that she was now in good hands that were able to provide the care she needed.

The next two days were the longest in Kate's life. The doctors could make her stay away from the hospital, but they couldn't make her rest. So she did the one thing she always did when she was upset—she cleaned! She washed the walls, scrubbed the floors—anything to keep her busy and keep her mind off the image of her helpless little girl lying in a hospital isolet with an IV tube dangling out of her arm.

During this time filled with anxiety and fear, one thought brought Kate great comfort and consistently remained in the back of her mind: "Nothing's going to happen that God and I can't handle together." She had heard the saying countless times before; but now, in the midst of this trying ordeal, it held new substance. It became an emotional anchor giving her much-needed stability during those stormy hours before Dana was finally able to come home to stay.

PRAYER: Lord God, Your arm is so strong and Your reach is so far that even when our children's lives are in peril, You are able to break through the wall of our fear and reach into the pit of our despair and touch us, strengthen us, and guide us. Thank You for the comfort that you alone can offer. Amen.

"Who Will You Become?"

Genesis 2:7. Then the LORD God formed man of dust from the ground, and breathed into his nostrils the breath of life; and man became a living being.

---

*T*hus Adam was created. The first of billions. Each person so alike, yet so different. What a miracle God accomplishes every time a sperm unites with an egg to create a unique individual who also bears the marks of the family to which he or she belongs!

"Who will you become?" I wonder as I watch a huge yawn overpower Christopher's tiny face. Some people say he looks like me. Will he be like me, or will he become more like his father? Now he is very small, very passive, very innocent. Soon he will be a person in his own right, expressing ideas and passions of his own.

"What kind of man will you grow up to be?" I wish I knew a magic formula that would ensure his future. One that would guarantee that he would mature into a good and righteous man of God, a person who will succeed in all he attempts because he lives his life as an expression of his love for the Lord. But there is no magic, nor are there any guarantees. For the same parents who conceived and reared Abel bore and nurtured Cain as well. How could two such different people be raised under the same roof?

My dear, sweet Christopher, how innocent and vulnerable you look as you blink and stare and gently move those tiny fingers. Who could know by looking at you that the seeds of both goodness and malice are sown deep in your soul? My awareness of the great responsibility that God has entrusted to me when he placed you in my care grows ever deeper. I am thankful that God allowed CT and me to participate in the creation of Christopher. I am awestruck by the challenge ahead.

PRAYER: Dear Lord, there is much that is hidden from us about our children. Only You hold the complete knowledge of who these children really are. Only You know the best they are meant to be. Lord, by Your Spirit open our eyes and ears that we might see them as the unique individuals You created. Give us the keys that will unlock the potential within them to become all that You intended. Show us how to help them mature into men and women of God. Amen.

A Reassuring Trip to
the Doctor

Ephesians 3:16. [I pray] that out of the treasures of his glory he may grant you strength and power through his Spirit in your inner being (NEB).

---

*T*oday was Christopher's first trip to the doctor's office. We have been home from the hospital just over a week, and already the pediatrician wanted to check up on his new little patient. Since Christopher is a breast-fed baby, the doctor wanted to make sure that he is getting the nourishment he requires and to see how both baby and mother were adjusting. One look at the dark circles under my eyes alerted him to the fact that I was having a rough time.

Even though I needed his encouragement and support, I was hesitant to share with him my struggles. I didn't want to appear as insecure and unsure as I felt. This seasoned veteran had seen hundreds of haggard new mothers stumble into his office, however; so it wasn't long before his warm smile and concerned questions allowed me to drop my guard. Soon I was asking question after question: "How is Christopher *really* doing? Is he gaining enough weight? His appetite wakes us both so frequently at night that I am worried that I am not producing enough milk and that he isn't getting enough to eat."

After patiently listening to all my questions and concerns, the doctor examined Christopher. "He appears to be quite a healthy and happy little boy," the doctor assured me. Then he directed me to pick up my son, who was naked but for his diaper, and follow him down the hall to the office scale, where he weighed Christopher. "There's the answer!" he exclaimed. "Christopher is what we call a 'gourmet grande'—he's gained a pound in little more than a week!"

The doctor explained that he was going through a growth spurt and that I could expect his feeding schedule to continue to be pretty demanding for another week or so. He assured me that it would let up eventually. For now, though, I was to continue to feed him on demand.

What a relief! I felt like a prisoner who had the date of her discharge set! Now I must look to the Lord for the deep strength needed to endure the rest of this trying time.

PRAYER: Dear God, thank you that no trial is unending. Strengthen us, down deep inside, by the power of Your Spirit that we might minister to Your children with joy. Amen.

The Special Spark

Ephesians 3:17b–19. With deep roots and firm foundations, may you be strong to grasp, with all God's people, what is the breadth and length and height and depth of the love of Christ, and to know it, though it is beyond knowledge (NEB).

CT and I knew something very special existed between us almost from our first encounter. It was a chance meeting through a mutual friend while we were both graduate students. Three friends decided to take a study break and go dancing for a few hours. They needed someone to complete their foursome, and our mutual friend said he knew just the person—me.

We had a marvelous time and decided to make this activity a weekly event. It was just what we needed to clear our minds and allow us to hit the books with renewed verve. The following week CT picked me up alone. As we talked and shared and laughed on the drive home, both of us were aware that already that spark existed—that one which alerts you to the fact that this could be serious! Although proceeding with extreme caution, we were married within the year.

When we began considering a family, I was concerned about what the addition of a third person might do to our relationship. With CT being the pastor of an active church, his time is spread very thin; so I guard jealously that portion set aside for the two of us alone. Would there be enough time, energy, and love to go around? I was afraid that our love would be diminished by the lack of time left for each other in the midst of caring for our child. What would become of that special spark? I didn't want to lose it.

After Christopher's arrival, we became aware that now, more than ever before, we were dependent upon the enabling work of the Holy Spirit. If we looked only to our own resources, our marriage could suffer. But as we turned to our shared faith and drew upon God's nutrients of patience and peace, we discovered that his love truly has no limits.

I am happy to report that that special spark still remains in our relationship. The love of our Lord has reached out and enveloped the three of us, expanding the capacities of our hearts as we reach out to grasp the love of Jesus. In Christ there is enough love to go around.

PRAYER: Father God, as we draw from our meager measure of human love and compassion, remind us that the ocean of love which exists in Your heart is there for our asking. Give us the courage to reach out and embrace it. Amen.

Thank Heaven for Our Mothers

Isaiah 40:11.

> He will take care of his flock like a shepherd;
> he will gather the lambs together
> and carry them in his arms;
> he will gently lead their mothers (TEV).

*C*hristopher's birth could not have occurred at a more unsettled point in our lives. CT had accepted a call to be the pastor of a parish in an eastern suburb of Cleveland. We purchased a snug little home well in advance of our arrival and made arrangements to stay with a family in our new congregation until the closing. Moving day was scheduled three weeks prior to my due date. That would allow ample time to unpack the necessities and to set up the nursery—or so we thought. The moving van arrived one day, and I went into labor the next!

Thank heaven for mothers! When we called my family in Washington State to share our wonderful and unexpected news, my mother hopped on the first flight she could get. While I recuperated in the hospital, she and CT worked night and day setting up furniture and unpacking boxes. What a blessing it was to come home to an organized house!

I don't remember ever feeling closer to my mother than I do right now. Our shared experience of motherhood has opened new doors of communication between us. I enjoy listening as she shares what she encountered as a new mother some twenty-nine years ago. I am thankful for her advice and expertise as a seasoned veteran in mothering skills. But what I appreciate most about her are who she is as a person and the integrity with which she lives her life.

Those two qualities about her were what allowed me to grow up believing that I could do and become whatever I chose to. Her *ways* showed the importance of being strong without becoming rigid, yet being vulnerable without becoming weak. I hope the Lord allows me to pass on this priceless gift to my son.

Tomorrow Mom leaves to go back to those who love her and need her on the West Coast. How will I manage without her help and advice? I draw courage from God's promises. He protects his little ones as he gathers them in his arms. Then he gently guides their mothers as they grapple with the new perplexities children bring into their lives.

PRAYER: Dear God, thank you for this special time of new discovery between us and our mothers. Thank you for the blessings of love and wisdom they share with us now when we need it most. Amen.

That First Smile

*A*nd the child
grew and became strong,
filled with wisdom; and the
favor of God was upon him.

Luke 2:40

The Strain on Other Relationships

Proverbs 17:17. Friends always show their love. What are brothers for if not to share trouble? (TEV).

---

*R*ugby used to sleep at the foot of our bed. He's our seventy-pound mutt who's as bouncy and lovable as his name implies. Before Christopher's arrival, he was "our baby." He was petted, played with, and pampered regularly. Rarely an evening passed that CT and I didn't take him for a long and rigorous walk.

Last week I noticed that he no longer sleeps in our bedroom. I guess he has had enough of being stepped on and stumbled over as I get up to tend to Christopher. I found him sleeping in a safe corner in the hallway, well out of my way. Poor Rugby. He certainly doesn't receive the attention he used to. Now it is Christopher who is showered with our love and devotion.

Noticing the change in Rugby causes me to pause and consider the state of my other relationships. At this point no one receives either the quality or quantity of attention I used to give to them. Letters from old friends lie unanswered, and conversations always seem to be interrupted. I wonder if my friends are feeling as taken for granted as Rugby seems to be?

Christopher requires an extraordinary amount of my attention. He is not a baby who sleeps much. Because of that, I find it difficult to maintain a quality conversation of any depth; equally difficult is initiating a phone call because a thousand other things clamor for my attention. When friends drop by, my concentration is divided. As one ear listens to my guests, the other ear listens for Christopher's baby sounds to make sure that he's okay. When they leave, I feel bad that I didn't give them the attention they deserved.

As delightful as motherhood is, I am saddened by the strain it places on my other relationships. I know that it is necessary while Christopher is still young and vulnerable. I just hope my friends understand.

PRAYER: Dear Lord, thank you for the many friends who touch and enrich our lives. Please give them the patience and understanding needed to withstand the upheaval in our relationships during this time of shifting responsibilities. Show us how to let them know that we still value their friendships and that our love has not diminished. Amen.

Prayer Time—
More Urgent and Sincere

Psalm 145:18-19.

> He is near to those who call to him,
>   who call to him with sincerity.
> He supplies the needs of those who honor him;
>   he hears their cries and saves them (TEV).

*E*arlier I talked about reassessing relationships. I took a long, hard look at how Christopher's needs have depleted the time and energy I used to reserve for friends and other family members.

Although I miss the deep sharing with friends, the relationship in which I feel the distance most acutely is that one which I share with my Lord, Jesus Christ. Gone are my scheduled times of prayer and daily devotions. Gone are my hours set aside for study. And, finally, gone are the lengthy periods of silence when I could just sit and listen for him with my whole being.

As frustrating and lonely as it feels sometimes, I know the Lord is teaching me to seek him out in new ways. I can no longer depend upon habit and discipline to sustain our relationship. My time is not mine alone to order as I please. It belongs to my son and his ever-present needs as well.

Our Scripture tells us that the Lord is near to those who call upon him with sincerity. My prayer time now is brief, but it is more urgent and sincere than ever. The moments I do have throughout the day I use to send up prayers which are like shooting arrows—swift and to the mark. I know he hears my voice because every once in a while his presence sneaks up on me when I least expect it. My heart senses his embrace, and then I know that he still cares; he still loves me.

I often feel distant from the God I love right now. But I know that as I honor the Lord in the ways that are available to me, he will hear my voice, draw ever closer, and supply all my needs.

PRAYER: Father God, continue to show us how to honor You and seek You in new ways. Much of what was comfortable and useful in our relationship with You no longer applies since our children entered our lives. Help us to prune away the spiritual dead wood so that the buds of new life might be nurtured and brought to fruition. Amen.

How Unique We All Are

Jeremiah 1:5a. "Before I formed you in the womb I knew you for my own" (NEB).

*A*n old Chinese proverb states, "Only one truly beautiful baby exists in the world, and it belongs to every mother."

I find that to be true. Before Christopher entered my life, I was one of those people who thought that all babies looked alike—like bald, prune-faced little people! They had no teeth, no eyebrows, and no personality. They were little creatures with squeaky cries and squinty eyes which rarely opened to take a peek at you. I could easily take them or leave them.

It's amazing how having my own child has changed my perception of things. Christopher was everything listed above—but he was the most beautiful baby I had ever seen! Yet the effect went well beyond just him, for now I saw other children in a new light as well. Just a few hours after Christopher's birth, as I gazed through the nursery window, the babies no longer looked all the same. Each one was unique—their facial features differed, their body sizes varied, even the expressions on their faces and the tenor of their cries were distinct.

God's love is so deep that I can't fathom it. I know that the love I feel for Christopher is only a dim reflection of the pure and total love God holds for each of his children. He loves us and relates to us as if each of us were his only child. How great is our God, that he could know me as his own unique child before my very conception!

PRAYER: We are thankful, Father God, for the special love You hold in Your heart for each one of us. We know that the deep and wondrous love which we feel for our children as mothers is a gift from You—from one parent to another. Thank you for this gracious blessing. Amen.

Protecting Our Husbands, Stunting Their Growth

Psalm 127:3–5a.
> Children are a gift from the LORD;
> they are a real blessing.
> The sons a man has when he is young
> are like arrows in a soldier's hand.
> Happy is the man who has many such arrows (TEV).

Meagan was crying again, and Linda felt that sick feeling deep in the pit of her stomach which she had come to know all too well. It was dinner time and Meagan was winding up for her usual fussy hour before being put to bed. Before James had a chance to console his daughter, Linda whisked her away to another room. As she jiggled and bounced and sang to Meagan, she thought, *Why now? Why do you have to cry NOW?*

Linda tried everything possible to present a peaceful house to James when he arrived home from a long day's work. She would feed Meagan early, play with her, and get her ready for bed so that her spirits would be up when her daddy came through the door. But try as Linda might, Meagan's tiny body had decided that early evening was the perfect time to exercise its lungs.

That sick feeling in Linda's stomach was not just a new mother's nervousness. She was trying to protect her husband from the discomfort caused by their baby's cry. She loved children and hoped to raise a substantial family. James, on the other hand, was not so sure. Before marriage, he had decided that his life would be fulfilling enough without experiencing fatherhood. After several years of marriage, he hesitantly agreed to start a family because he loved Linda deeply and knew how much it meant to her.

Now Linda was afraid that if James's experience of Meagan wasn't perfect, he would regret their decision and choose not to expand their family any further. But her very fear was stunting James's growth as a father by not allowing him the opportunity to console his child in the midst of her discomfort or ill-temper.

For once James was allowed to experience the full spectrum of fatherhood, his love for children blossomed. He has grown to become one of the most sensitive, nurturing and loving fathers I know. Now with four daughters instead of one, he is filled with joy at the rich blessings that each brings into his life.

PRAYER: Thank you, Lord, that You not only hold our children in the palm of Your hand, but You hold our spouses as well. Help us to trust You as we see our husbands struggle with their new roles as fathers. Show us how to give them the space they need to grow into their new responsibilities. Amen.

Age-Old Anxiety and Ever-Present Strength

Exodus 2:2–3. And she bore him a son. When she saw what a fine baby he was, she hid him for three months. But when she could not hide him any longer, she took a basket made of reeds and covered it with tar to make it watertight. She put the baby in it and then placed it in the tall grass at the edge of the river (TEV).

Jochebed gave birth at a troubled point in her people's history. Fearing the sheer number of Hebrews in his land, Pharaoh had placed them in bondage. Seeing that this did not diminish their population, he later decreed that all their male babies were to be put to death. The same nation who had once saved Jacob's family from famine by welcoming them into their country now turned from friend to captor. It was during this perilous time that Moses was born.

Jochebed could not let her newborn son be drowned as Pharaoh had mandated. What anxiety she must have experienced as she kept her son in hiding, living in constant fear that the sound of soldiers' heavy footsteps might find their way to her door!

Knowing that Jochebed could no longer conceal the cries of her child, I can only speculate at the plan she began to devise. She had heard that Pharaoh's daughter was a kind-hearted woman, and now she chose to count upon her compassion. Who would question the love for a child expressed by one of the royal family? Who would dare take him from her?

So early one morning Jochebed placed her beloved son in a basket which she had carefully sealed with tar in order to keep its precious cargo afloat. Then, with the first glimmerings of dawn upon the horizon, she stole down to the banks of the Nile and placed the basket amidst the reeds near the place where Pharaoh's daughter bathed.

God was faithful to Jochebed. Not only was Moses' life saved, but Jochebed was allowed to suckle and care for her son during his first years of life.

We, like Jochebed, live in troubled times. Although not physically enslaved, it is easy to be oppressed by the tyranny of fear—fear that our children might become one of the thousands of those who are missing in our country, fear that they will be abused when left in the care of someone we trust. Hearing account after account of such instances sometimes causes me to feel very helpless, to feel there is no escape, no safe haven for my child.

But I take courage from the story of Jochebed. She did not allow her fear to paralyze her. Instead, she took action. She sought the Lord, devised a plan, and then entrusted Moses to the hands of God as she carried it through.

PRAYER: Father God, please give us the courage to face our fears and the sickness in our society as Jochebed did. Then share with us the gift of Your wisdom that we might devise wise plans which will protect our children. And, finally, Lord, after we have done all that we can, help us to continue to trust You. Amen.

A Smile Reveals God's Gifts

James 1:16–17a. Make no mistake, my friends. All good giving, every perfect gift, comes from above, from the Father of the lights of heaven (NEB).

There it is! That crooked toothless grin I've been waiting for. I've watched for it since Christopher drew his first breath of life. There have been moments before now when I thought he was right on the verge. The corners of his mouth would curl for an instant, then return to their usual state, showing little emotion. You may call it coincidence or say it's only gas, but today he looked up into my face and broke out with a full-fledged smile! I thought my very heart would melt with joy.

This is one of those moments a mother treasures for a lifetime. One little smile, and somehow all the wakeful nights, dirty diapers, and crusty shoulders are worth it. As she watches her child's first expression of joy, she begins to understand the purpose behind all of her self-sacrifice.

That first smile revealed a bit more of Christopher's character. It acted like a small window which allowed me to peek a little deeper into his developing personality. He is no longer a mysterious stranger who expresses only hunger and discomfort. A whole new dimension of his being is beginning to open up. He will soon be a person with a sense of humor all his own.

A simple little smile. Who could have guessed it would mean so much or bring such joy? Only the mother of the child herself! My child is a gift from God, a treasure from his storehouse beyond all earthly value.

PRAYER: Thank you, dear Lord, for this gift which surprises! Just when we feel we have given and given until we can give no more, in an instant You recharge our energy by flooding our souls with new joy and purpose. Thank you, Lord, for surprising us with Your love through the perfect gift of a child. Amen.

A TV's Thievery of Time

Joshua 24:15. "But if serving the LORD seems undesirable to you, then choose for yourselves this day whom you will serve, whether the gods your forefathers served beyond the River, or the gods of the Amorites, in whose land you are living. But as for me and my household, we will serve the LORD" (NIV).

Today I turned off the TV. It has been Christopher's and my constant companion since we arrived home from the hospital, and I fear that we are becoming "television addicts"! I find that I leave it on hour after hour because I like to hear the sound of another adult voice in the house. It also provides a distraction while I struggle to accomplish some of the more tedious chores of motherhood. Although the TV may seem helpful, one thing I've discovered is that it helps my day pass more quickly *because* it is a great and subtle thief of my time and attention.

Sometimes at day's end I feel anesthetized and wonder where the hours have gone and why I haven't accomplished more. I didn't watch a movie in the afternoon or a string of soap operas. For me it is the few minutes here and there that really add up. I'll sit down in front of the TV for a quick cup of coffee and find twenty minutes later that I haven't moved an inch. While folding clothes or finishing some other chore, a program will capture my attention. After the task is completed, I find myself tarrying just until the next commercial— or to the end of the program—before I move on.

What's wrong with relaxing a little and letting the day go by at a slower pace? Nothing, if such has been a conscious decision. But I allow a machine to steal the only commodities I really control—my time and my thoughts. Instead of focusing my mind on the things of the Lord, I allow it to drift with the whims of this world as expressed through the media.

I fear that by spending so much time under the influence of television, I am beginning to serve the "Amorites" of the land and their values instead of the Lord whom I love. I am also concerned about the example I am setting for Christopher. By being more selective in what I watch today, I am making my choice: as for me and my family, we shall serve the Lord!

PRAYER: Dear God, help us to be good stewards of our time. Show us how to serve You in all that we do and allow Your presence to envelop our homes. Amen.

When the Excitement Dies

Lamentations 3:22-23.

> The steadfast love of the LORD never ceases,
>   his mercies never come to an end;
> they are new every morning;
>   great is thy faithfulness.

*I*t was another in a string of endless days and sleepless nights. The small hours of the morning found me rocking back and forth, trying to comfort that restless little bundle huddled in my arms. "Sleep—sleep! Oh, Lord, why won't this baby sleep?"

I could hear CT's rhythmic breathing in the next room, and I resented the fact that his night would pass uninterrupted. It seemed as though the whole world enjoyed the luxury of peaceful slumber—except me.

As I sat rocking in the dark, the tears began to fall. I realized another change had occurred. The adrenalin accompanying Christopher's birth and the excitement of my new charge as a mother were gone. At that moment I felt no joy, no wonder—only exhaustion, resentment, and a sense of helplessness. "Lord, will I ever step out from under this weary burden of fatigue?"

With dawn approaching, Christopher and I finally dozed. When I awoke, the nursery was filled with the brilliant light of a glorious August morning. Refreshed by my short nap, I again realized the Lord's deep abiding gift of love. Although obscured by the darkness of exhaustion and despair, it still remained as constant and as strong as the Giver of the gift himself.

As I gazed upon the sweet, peaceful face of my son, I was reminded of God's promise. His love cannot be exhausted. It is renewed every morning. As I turn to God and allow the dawn of his understanding to appear on the horizon of my heart, I can again see that his deep, abiding love has stood fast, strengthening me from deep within.

PRAYER: Dear Lord, in those desperate tired hours, show us by Your Spirit how to draw strength from Your ever-flowing stream of love. Amen.

The Weight of Family Demands

Colossians 1:11. We are praying, too, that you will be filled with his mighty, glorious strength so that you can keep going no matter what happens—always full of the joy of the Lord (*The Living Bible*).

CT and I had another fight last night. He came to bed fairly late, and ready for a little romance. Exhausted after days and nights with little sleep, I showed no interest. With backs turned toward each other in icy silence, the cold war was on.

He understands with his mind that my lack of interest does not reflect a diminished love and concern for him. He knows the real culprits. He's read about the hormonal imbalance in a woman's body after birth, and he sees the exhaustion in my eyes. When I explain that it is sometimes difficult to be physically intimate with him after spending most of the day with Christopher in my arms, he understands my need to be alone. Yet although his *reasoning* may understand why his request is met with a no instead of a yes, his *emotions* rebel. He is feeling that his needs are not only displaced by Christopher but also forgotten by me.

It seems as though the needs of the two males in my house are about to crash head-on, and I am to be the point of their collision! Right now, I don't think I could survive the impact, for I'm struggling to keep my head above my own needs and difficulties. When I depend upon my own strength, I feel as if I am going to collapse under the weight of the emotional and physical demands of my family. Yet when I turn to God's Word, I am reminded that through Christ we are not only enabled to meet the challenges placed in our paths, but the joy of the Lord is our companion, uplifting both our hearts and spirits ar.d strengthening us as we move on.

PRAYER: Lord Jesus, as we spend our day responding to the cries of our children, let us not forget the sometime silent cry of our mate as well. Fill our marriages with Your understanding and love. Amen.

When I Am Sick

Isaiah 43:1–3. Don't be afraid, for I have ransomed you; I have called you by name; you are mine. When you go through deep waters and great trouble, I will be with you. When you go through rivers of difficulty, you will not drown! When you walk through the fire of oppression, you will not be burned up—the flames will not consume you. For I am the Lord your God, your Savior, the Holy One of Israel (*The Living Bible*).

I must be exhausted, I thought as I sat across the breakfast table from our houseguests with my head propped up by my hand. Good friends from Connecticut had stopped to spend the weekend with us on their way to see family in Michigan. Their stay had been filled with sightseeing and late-night chats. As we shared their last meal with us, my head began to swim, the room began to spin, and the kitchen floor moved like the deck of an ocean-going ship! I guessed that finally I had really overdone things and had worn my poor body out.

After saying goodbye to those special people, I headed upstairs with Christopher, hoping that both of us could take a nap. Soon my eyes began to burn with fever. I took my temperature, and the mercury climbed to 103 degrees. At that point I knew I had something which rest alone could not cure.

I called the doctor, and from my symptoms she diagnosed mastitis. She called the pharmacy for medication that CT would be able to pick up, and then prescribed bedrest, fever-reducing medicine, and heat packs. It was also suggested that I should find someone to help care for my family.

Now I am not a very good patient. I feel guilty taking a twenty-minute nap, let alone going to bed for several days. Being a newcomer to Cleveland and having no family in the area, I knew no one I felt comfortable in asking for help. So, with CT's help, we struggled along on our own.

Thank heavens my condition wasn't serious. But the experience made me feel vulnerable. Being a mother to one so small, I couldn't afford to be sick. It's not like a job, where I could call into the office for a day of sick leave. No, Christopher depends on me for his total care. I haven't just my own health to consider but his as well. I found myself confronted with the realization that I am not in control, that at any time I could lose my health or home, and then what would happen to my child?

I know that when I am ill, fear and depression walk hand in hand. Left to my own understanding, I could easily have been swept into a morass of gloom. But God's Word spoke assurance in the midst of my human fear. Because of his love, he accompanies me even in the depths of my own despair. As I look to him, I know that whatever awaits me will not overwhelm me. Rather, his Spirit will enable me to be triumphant, no matter how great the trial.

PRAYER: Lord God, even in the depths of our own despair You are there waiting for us. Your Spirit makes it possible for us to keep our heads above whatever befalls us. And we can be sure that You will do the same for our children. Help us to trust You and not fall prey to the fears of life. Keep us ever mindful of just how loving and powerful our God is. Amen.

A Sojourn
Near Peaceful Waters

Psalm 23:2b-3.
> [He] leads me beside the waters of peace;
>   he renews life within me,
> and for his name's sake guides me in the
>   right path (NEB).

A cool breeze gently rustled the leaves of the big oak tree in our backyard as it meandered through the branches and then softly swept through an open window into the nursery. It had been one of those sticky-hot summer days, the kind that, unless you are stretched out at the beach somewhere or sipping a cool drink at poolside, can make you cranky and miserable. We had all suffered from the effects of the heat; so I welcomed the wind's refreshing touch in the darkness of the very early morn.

All was at peace. CT finally slept soundly after tossing and turning through the discomfort of the late evening heat. Rugby curled up for a short snooze at my feet. And Christopher, with his tummy full after a 3 A.M. feeding, slept securely on my shoulder with his fuzzy little head nestled up against my neck.

Ah, a quiet moment! I would not have expected myself to welcome it at such an odd hour, but God knows my needs much better than I. My whole being had been crying out for a sojourn near our Lord's peaceful waters. The many transitions and adjustments I was experiencing not only brought upheaval to my relationships and lifestyle but caused turmoil in my soul and spirit as well.

There, while I rocked by the window enjoying the cool caress of the morning breeze, I experienced the restoring power of the Holy Spirit. It was as though my soul had been allowed to quench its thirst after a long and arduous journey. As I drank in the refreshing peace of the Lord, I felt God at work, renewing the very life within me.

PRAYER: Thank you, Lord, for those quiet moments alone with You. They seem to be hard to find with our new responsibilities, but now we need them more than ever. Show us how to seek them out in the midst of our busy day. Amen.

Finding New Meaning in Humble Duties

Romans 12:16. Have the same concern for everyone. Do not be proud, but accept humble duties. Do not think of yourselves as wise (TEV).

---

*T*he shadows were growing long as evening approached on a bright but crisp October afternoon. The church picnic had been a great success. The smell of corn roasting over an open fire mingled in the air with the sounds of laughter and lighthearted conversation.

As some of the men and older children finished their last game of touch football, I took Christopher inside the church for a final diaper change before the drive home. When I reached the church nursery, I found Terri standing at the window while Amy, her two-and-a-half-month-old daughter, slept in one of the cribs. At this point in her young life, Amy was a baby who spent most of her days in tears.

As I changed Christopher's diaper, Terri shared how trying it was to be home all day with Amy. "Just look at him!" she exclaimed as she pointed out the window at her husband playing football. "His life hasn't changed a bit since Amy was born. He still goes to work every day; he sleeps every night; he plays golf on the weekend with his buddies." There was an edge to her voice, and I could see the resentment in her face. Terri was a gifted professional in her own right with a promising career. Now she found herself home all day with a crying baby—feeling alone and taken for granted.

Stepping from a rewarding and quickly rising career to staying at home with a temperamental infant was a staggering transition for Terri. And she found little support at attempting that step from those who surrounded her. Many of her friends and co-workers could not understand her decision. They seemed to remind her at every opportunity of all the "benefits" she was missing by the decision she had made. It was hard for them to comprehend her choice to put the financial rewards and prestige which her job offered "on hold" while accepting the challenge to decipher and respond to the needs of a fussy child.

Yet Christ brings new meaning to this choice. As the weeks and months passed, Terri gained new insight into the purpose of all those difficult and tedious hours spent with her unhappy daughter. She began to see that when she accepted the humble duties of caring for Amy, God called her beyond the present. Through those seemingly meaningless tasks, he allowed her to become his partner in preparing her child for the future.

PRAYER: Lord, open our eyes to see the rewards of the new challenges You have placed before us. Help us see Your purpose in those endless, humble chores. Amen.

Loving Thoughts, Critical Actions

Romans 7:15, 25b. I do not understand what I do; for I don't do what I would like to do, but instead I do what I hate. This, then, is my condition: on my own I can serve God's law only with my mind, while my human nature serves the law of sin (TEV).

*T*his has been a difficult day. Sometimes I feel as though I am riding an emotional roller coaster. While standing at the sink this morning washing the breakfast dishes, I experienced such tender and loving thoughts about what a wonderful husband and father CT is. Yet when he unexpectedly popped in for lunch, along with his meal I dished up large helpings of criticism and anger.

I can identify with the apostle Paul. I *don't* understand my own actions. Why is it that when I feel such loving thoughts and emotions for my husband, I wound up barraging him instead with anger, guilt, and resentment? I feel so picky and selfish. Part of me wants to minister to his needs, while a stronger part clearly wants him to pamper and care for me!

Today the precious gift of himself which CT offered through his conversation and presence was not enough. I would have preferred to see him come through the door with a dozen roses and a bottle of perfume. When it didn't happen, instead of honestly sharing with him my needs and desires in a way that would have allowed him to respond, my sinful, selfish side showed its ugly face. My disappointment turned into anger and overshadowed the loving person I wanted to be.

I am grateful that the Bible is filled with the witness of real people. I appreciate that Paul cared enough about the Christian community to share with us his own struggle with sin.

PRAYER: Thank you, Lord, that at the end of days like today, when we feel like such failures, we can, like Paul, throw ourselves on Your mercy. There, through the loving forgiveness of Jesus Christ, we find release from guilt and the power of sin. Amen.

Balancing the "Mary" and "Martha" Within

Luke 10:38–42. As Jesus and his disciples were on their way, he came to a village where a woman named Martha opened her home to him. She had a sister called Mary, who sat at the Lord's feet listening to what he said. But Martha was distracted by all the preparations that had to be made. She came to him and asked, "Lord, don't you care that my sister has left me to do the work by myself? Tell her to help me!"

"Martha, Martha," the Lord answered, "you are worried and upset about many things, but only one thing is needed. Mary has chosen what is better, and it will not be taken away from her" (NIV).

---

*A*lice sat curled up in her favorite overstuffed chair in a sunny corner of her living room. She was enjoying a rare moment spent in Bible study and devotions. As Alice read the passage above, she felt like Jesus was speaking directly to her when he said, "You are worried and upset about many things." Her life was filled with a great amount of busy work these days.

Alice was a "Mary" at heart. She was a student by nature and loved to spend hours at the Master's feet. Before Caitlyn's birth she regularly spent much time in Bible study and prayer. She was also a good listener and always had time to share a cup of coffee with the many people who sought out her counsel and companionship.

Now her days seemed consumed by menial yet necessary

tasks. It was beyond her imagination that someone as small as Caitlyn could dirty so much laundry! She was having a difficult time learning how to roll up her sleeves and become a "Martha" when she had always taken such joy in being a "Mary."

Since becoming a mother, Alice has gained a new appreciation for all the "Marthas" in her life. Before, she couldn't understand what she perceived as being their preoccupation with schedules, organization, and household chores. Now she knows that if she doesn't keep on top of things, the sometimes unpredictable responsibilities of motherhood can quickly pile up and seem insurmountable. And when she feels overwhelmed and out of control, their family life suffers because she provides the continuity which holds the emotional makeup of their family together. More than ever, she now realizes the blessings a well-balanced life can hold, both for herself and for her family.

PRAYER: Dear Jesus, open our minds that we might understand the purpose which You have placed in every moment and every task of our day. Help us to enjoy the presence of Your Spirit in all things. Please enable us to appreciate both the "Mary" and the "Martha" which You have placed within us and show us how to keep them in balance. Amen.

Discerning God's Gifts Within Our Children

Luke 2:40. The child grew and became strong; he was full of wisdom, and God's blessings were upon him (TEV).

---

*L*ook at those little fingers. Christopher can wrap a whole fist of them around just one of mine. Although his hands are small, I feel a strengthening grip developing. That grip causes me to stop and wonder at the potential which lies within my son and to question whether or not I am made of the right stuff to help him become all that God intends.

Will I have eyes to recognize an emerging talent, hidden like a rose among the thorns? Will I have the patience to allow that flower to blossom in its own time? Or will I be a pushy mother, forcing Christopher into areas he is not ready to go?

What a blessing it is to be a partner with God, working together with him to call out the gifts he has placed deep within my son! I am thankful that this responsibility does not rest upon CT's and my shoulders alone. I pray Christopher will continue to grow in strength, wisdom, and God's blessings.

PRAYER: Creator God, our children grow in many ways. You have placed enormous potential within each one of them. Yet each is different from all the rest. Help us to affirm them as unique individuals. In the midst of all their potential, help us to distinguish those few gifts that are specially from You for this particular child. And grant us a sense of timing that will allow us to nurture our children instead of pushing them. Amen.

A Promise of God's Closeness

Psalm 34:4, 6.
> I prayed to the LORD, and he answered me;
> he freed me from all my fears.
> The helpless call to him, and he answers;
> he saves them from all their troubles (TEV).

*D*arla opened the door to the nursery to check on her son one last time before she turned in for the night. There was an autumn chill in the air, and as she pulled an extra blanket up around Timmy's neck and tucked it under his chin, he released a contented sigh. She paused for a moment, watching the steady movement of Timmy's breathing, then whispered, "Oh, God, how can I entrust the most treasured gift You've ever given me to the care of a complete stranger?"

Darla would be returning to work soon, and it was time to arrange for Timmy's child care. Who could she get to watch him? She had no family in the area—both she and her husband had followed their careers to a city far from home. She thought that perhaps one of their friends would care for him but soon found out that they had jobs and obligations of their own. It looked like Darla was going to have to find a stranger to watch her son, and that realization filled her with fear. She was uncomfortable in leaving him with an acquaintance for any length of time, let alone trusting him to a stranger! It seemed as though every night on the news she was hearing of more and more children being abused in what had appeared to be safe situations. She did not want Timmy added to the statistics.

How can Darla guarantee the safety of her child? How will she find the right person to care for Timmy? There are no simple answers, but God does promise to be close to those who call upon him in all sincerity. Darla felt it was time to look to the Lord for her answers and trust that he would bring those special people into Timmy's life who would love and care for him in her absence. She knew that there is only one place upon which our trust can rest without fear of disappointment: in the God who holds our lives, moment, by moment, in his very hands.

PRAYER: Dear Lord, help us make wise decisions as we look for people to care for our children. Please protect them in our absence. And most of all, may they always feel the loving arms of their Father God surrounding them. Amen.

Contentment with the Present

Matthew 6:34: "Do not worry about tomorrow; it will have enough worries of its own. There is no need to add to the troubles each day brings" (TEV).

The fading warmth of the evening sun felt good as I sat rocking the glider on the deck in our backyard. The sun was beginning to set, and as it did, the western sky turned that beautiful shade of sky-blue-pink which only early summer holds. This is one of my favorite times of the day. Dinner is over, the dishes are done, and CT has returned to the office. Christopher and I now share an opportunity to relax and enjoy each other's company.

This must be the best time in my life, I thought as I watched the glorious sunset and held a content little bundle in my arms. The special joy that Christopher brings to me warms my heart in much the same way as the summer sun warms my body. The peace I feel when he is at peace runs long and deep, as if I've been brought closer to the source of all good things. And the love I feel is different from any other I've ever known. This must be an inkling of what our Father God feels when he showers his love upon us and then discovers that his children are returning part of that blessing to him in their own childlike fashion.

It's easy for me to allow that joy, peace, and love to go unnoticed much of the time. My life is often full of noise and activity, and I am always racing into the future. I am looking ahead so much of the time that I often miss the many blessings which the present holds.

I am thankful for this quiet moment when I can appreciate Christopher for who he is right now, without concerning myself with his future. He truly is a gift from God.

PRAYER: Thank you, Lord, for the many joys which You sprinkle upon the present. Help us not to be so forward-looking that we miss the blessings each day holds. And for today, Lord, thank you especially for the warmth and joy found in the simple act of holding a contented child. Amen.

The Battle with Self-Love

Psalm 37:5.

Commit your way to the LORD ;
trust in him, and he will act.

What a depressing sight! I thought as I took a long, hard look at myself in the mirror. *Christopher is two months old, and my stomach still shakes like a bowl of jello and feels like a lump of bread dough; and I have twenty pounds more to lose—all of which are located in the wrong places! I don't know how CT can stand to look at me. I'm certainly not the 106-pound bride he married three years ago.*

With that gloomy self-assessment, I headed for the kitchen to raise a white flag of surrender to my dieting dilemma in the form of a bowl of "tin-roof" ice cream. I always turn to ice cream when I'm feeling depressed. As I sat cross-legged on the couch with the bowl and spoon in my hand, I began to think about how my bathroom scale dictates the way I feel about myself and treat myself. When my weight is up, I feel ugly, and I act ugly. Then, to prove that I *am* ugly, I eat more, which makes my weight go even higher, and the cycle goes on and on.

When I feel down on myself, I find it hard to believe that other people can feel differently about me, and that difficulty affects my marriage. Sometimes I get so trapped in the material that I have difficulty believing that CT could love me in the same way he did when I was slim. I lose sight of the fact that he sees me through the eyes of real love. So when CT compliments me or expresses his love for me in another way, I can't receive it because *I* don't believe I am lovable. Instead of saying thank you for the compliments and enjoying his love, I slough them off or make light of them. That hurts his feelings because he gets the message loud and clear that I think his affection is shallow and his compliments are meaningless niceties.

But I am blessed with a husband who possesses a persistent love for his wife. He continues to reach out to me again and again until I must surrender to his sincerity and support. He loves me just the way I am, but he also wants to help me be the best I can be. So he goes before the Lord with me in prayer, committing my goals and desires to God. Together we trust that God will act to enable me to become what I think he is calling me to be and not to allow our bathroom scale or some fashion magazine to dictate my self-worth. CT trusts also that if my goals are a little off target, our gracious Lord will adjust my aim to become exactly what is in keeping with his will for my life.

PRAYER: Lord Jesus, help us to see ourselves through Your eyes and to remember that Your love never wavers. Show us how to allow Your love to illumine our goals so that we might become all that You intend us to be, instead of being trapped by earthly standards. Amen.

Numbering the Days,
the Tasks, . . .

Psalm 90:12. Teach us to number our days and recognize how few they are; help us to spend them as we should (*The Living Bible*).

What did I ever do with all my time before Christopher was born?" I asked as I looked at the clutter around me. There were dishes in the sink, a two-month-old stack of papers and bills on the kitchen counter, and a pile of correspondence waiting to be answered on my desk. And they were but a few of the backlog of tasks waiting for my attention. "Will I ever be organized again?" I wondered.

Lately, I am lucky to keep up with the laundry and run the vacuum now and then, let alone stay on top of all the rest of my family, church, and business responsibilities. Christopher not only keeps me up at night; he keeps me busy during the day as well. Dear Lord, please let my next child be a good sleeper!

The very fact that the clutter and disorganization annoy me is a cue that it is time to get back to normal. What's the secret to juggling it all? So many things have piled up that the task seems insurmountable.

I need God's wisdom to help me prioritize all the unfinished business and incomplete tasks in my life. It is time to choose what I ought to tackle first and what can be left undone a little longer. I want to order my days in a way that reflects his wisdom and love. I know that if I keep my mind on God's priorities first, all the rest will fall into place.

PRAYER: Lord Jesus, sometimes we get so caught up in the business of raising a new family that we forget that the days we have to spend are numbered. Help us to be good stewards of the time which You have graciously allotted. Enable us to keep our homes in good order while we shower our children with the love and attention they need. Help us to ferret out the responsibilities that could best be taken on by someone else, while meeting those which You have specially appointed for us to do. Dear God, teach us how to live loving and balanced lives. Amen.

Lost in the Shuffle

Jeremiah 31:3.
I have loved you with an everlasting love,
and so I still maintain my faithful love for you
(*Jerusalem Bible*).

*A*llen's dinner plate rested before him while he waited for his wife to be seated and share in their evening meal. He knew that considerable effort had gone into its preparation; so he didn't want to start without Laura. She had been waylaid by Katie again. It seemed as though every time they sat down to a hot meal, Katie needed her pants changed. Tonight was no exception. Just as Laura took the food off the stove and set it on the table, Katie began to howl. As Laura marched Katie upstairs, Allen looked around him at his tepid dinner, then quietly growled, "Cold peas again!"

All day long Allen had looked forward to the dinner hour. There was no one's company he enjoyed more than Laura's, and they had traditionally set dinner time aside for each other. They would eat their meal leisurely, discussing the events of the day. Laura possessed great insight, and Allen valued her opinions. But all that had changed with the advent of Katie. Now he spent most of his meal sitting alone while Laura tended to Katie's needs. The short time Laura did sit at the table was spent gobbling a cold meal. Allen found the incidental table talk which remained to be very frustrating and unfulfilling. Laura seemed forever distracted and her attention divided.

They no longer enjoyed the privilege of focusing exclusively on each other.

Allen's feelings were hurt. Although he knew his desires would have to take a back seat to Katie's needs—particularly while she was young—he didn't expect to feel this lost in the shuffle. He was surprised to find their lives as radically changed as they were for such a long period of time. He now found himself squarely facing the fact that their lives were never going to be the same again, and he wasn't quite sure how to handle it.

Allen loved Katie very much, but to be honest he really missed the old days spent with just Laura. He no longer felt "special" in Laura's eyes. He felt more like a burden—like extra dishes to wash and additional laundry to do. Because he didn't want to be more of a burden, he couldn't bring himself to share his feelings with her. He was feeling lonely and unloved.

Allen's new reserve signaled to Laura that something was wrong. She had assumed that he knew how her love for him had deepened as she watched him selflessly step aside so that she might have more emotional energy to spend on their daughter. She had also taken for granted his experience of God's constant love. She had grown so busy with Katie that she had neglected to share with him her true feelings. She knew that it was time to find a new way to communicate both her appreciation and God's ever-present love to her spouse.

PRAYER: Creator God, thank you that no matter how *we* feel, we are always special to You. As our lives are being abruptly rearranged and we feel lost and all alone, help us to remember Your complete and unchanging love. Amen.

A "Blown" Day?

James 4:13-14. Look here, you people who say, "Today or tomorrow we are going to such and such a town, stay there a year, and open up a profitable business." How do you know what is going to happen tomorrow? For the length of your lives is as uncertain as the morning fog—now you see it; soon it is gone (*The Living Bible*).

My day was all planned. I had several appointments to keep and a number of errands to run. Today I was going to tie up all the loose ends which had been hanging over my head for weeks. I even got up early to make sure I could stay on schedule and arranged for a baby-sitter to watch Christopher so that I could accomplish my tasks quickly. This was going to be a productive day!

I finished packing the diaper bag, picked up Christopher, and made my way to the car. There, I placed him in his car seat and buckled him in. "Perfect. I'm right on schedule," I observed with a smile as I returned to the house for one last item; but little did I know what lay just ahead!

When I returned to the car, I found Christopher screaming as he sat in the midst of what is called in our house "*a major blow-out!*" There was poop everywhere—he was covered from head to toe, and the car seat was a mess! Needless to say, by the time I bathed Christopher, cleaned up the car, and washed and dried the fabric cover for his car seat, the morning had disappeared!

How frustrating! It seems as though I can never get ready early enough to arrive at an appointment on time now that Christopher is a part of my life. He either spits up on me or poops on me or needs something else just as I'm going out the door.

At times like this it is all too easy to see my son as an inconvenience instead of a ten-week-old little boy who needs my love and care. Lord Jesus, help me to remember that Christopher is one of the "purposes" that You have placed in my life and not just one of the "problems."

PRAYER: Dear God, sometimes it is difficult for us to provide a loving presence for our children, especially when the situations they present can be quite exasperating! Grant us the patience we need to provide the kind of loving care they desperately need. Amen.

A Congregation Promises
Support

Isaiah 54:13. And all thy children shall be taught of the LORD; and great shall be the peace of thy children (KJV).

*T*oday was a day filled with promises. As both sets of grandparents, CT, and I stood with Christopher before the baptismal fount, we joined with God's people in baptizing our son.*

CT and I promised to do our best to enable Christopher to be a disciple of Christ: one who obeys his words and shows his love. That is quite a responsibility to carry out! Often when I think of baptism, I remember the warm feelings, the beautiful babies present, and the wonderful promises that God holds out for his children. I too easily forget that in baptism I make promises to those children as well.

I am grateful that God places us in a Christian family, the church. For today, on this steamy morning in June, I am reminded that CT and I are not the only ones who will help Christopher grow up to be a man of God. His extended Christian family—our loving congregation—promised to join us in our efforts to help him understand the gospel and all that Christ commands. They promised to be in fellowship with him and to help strengthen his ties to the family of God.

I have participated in many baptisms as a parishioner; yet for some reason I didn't expect the baptism of my own child to be such a moving experience. It caught me by surprise. To hear CT, as pastor, speak in very simple terms to Christopher of the

Good News of the gospel and of all the benefits it holds, and to hear him do it in a way so intimate that it was as if only the two of them were present, brought tears to my eyes. Jesus Christ is already personally involved with Christopher's life. Seeing the evidence of this in one so small, so vulnerable, so incapable of response demonstrated to me that the "personal" aspect of my relationship with Christ does not depend upon my own ability to reach out for God. In the baptism of my son I see Christ reaching out to his children long before we are ever capable of reaching back. What a loving God we have!

PRAYER: Thank you, Lord, that Your Word is filled with promises made to Your people. We know that we can count on their fulfillment because the very Creator of the universe has given them to us. Enable us to keep the promises we have made to love, teach and disciple our children, that their lives might be filled with Your peace. Amen.

*In some traditions, instead of baptizing an infant, the parents and congregation bring the child before God in a service of infant dedication.

Seeking God's Guidance

*T*hy word is a
*lamp to guide my feet and
a light on my path.*

Psalm 119:105, NEB

Thoughts Upon Returning
to Work

Proverbs 16:9. We should make plans—counting on God to direct us (*The Living Bible*).

Jennifer was bundled up and ready to go. Gail, already loaded down with bottles, baby food, diapers, toys, and an extra change of clothes ("just in case!"), picked up her little girl and somehow made her way out the door and down the walk to the car. As Gail pulled out of her drive after loading the car, she quickly ran down her mental list of "things to remember." Assured that the diaper bag was properly equipped and that she really was ready for work, she headed for the sitter's house.

After dropping Jennifer with Mrs. Franklin, the new sitter, and explaining to her Jennifer's usual routine, Gail began her thirty-minute commute to the office. As she pulled onto the thruway, she relaxed a little and began wondering what this day held for both Jennifer and herself.

This was her first day back at the office since Jennifer's birth. Gail felt excited and a little apprehensive but looked forward to seeing her friends and co-workers again. She welcomed the challenge of her work and more than ever felt that she would appreciate a scheduled routine. Although Gail felt her day held much excitement and joy, she wasn't too sure about Jennifer's.

"Will she miss me? Will Mrs. Franklin remember all of my instructions? Will Jennifer be safe and happy? Will she feel loved?" These questions and many more gnawed at Gail's heart as she drove.

For Gail, like many women, the choice between staying home with her child and returning to work was a difficult and complicated one to make. Her decision to return to her job was one that had been made after much prayer and considerable discussion with her husband. Together they sought God's wisdom as to what would be best for their family as a whole. After seeking God's leading to the best of their ability, their decision had been made. Gail would return to work once a loving sitter could be found. After interviewing several people, they felt that Mrs. Franklin was the answer to their prayers.

As she drove, Gail lifted her concerns for her daughter to the Lord, and she felt his assurance. She had sought his wisdom, and he had generously given it. As she entered the office parking lot, she was confident that her trust in God had been well placed. She must now have faith in the decision that he had helped her reach.

PRAYER: Thank you, God, that you share your wisdom generously. Help us always to seek Your mind, and then grant us Your loving guidance. Amen.

Loving with an Open Hand

Read 1 Samuel 1:1-28.

1 Samuel 1:27-28. "I asked him for this child, and he gave me what I asked for. So I am dedicating him to the LORD. As long as he lives, he will belong to the LORD" (TEV).

---

*H*annah was a desperate woman. Her desire for a child had grown so great over the years that not even the love and devotion of her husband could comfort her. Barren in an age when a woman's worth was measured by the offspring she produced, Hannah could bear the humiliation no longer. Weeping bitterly, she made a promise to God, "LORD Almighty, look at me, your servant! See my trouble and remember me! Don't forget me! If you give me a son, I promise that I will dedicate him to you for his whole life . . ."(1 Samuel 1:11,TEV).

God heard her desperate cry, and it wasn't long before she discovered the new life growing within her womb. Hannah must have felt the warmth of God's smile on the day of Samuel's birth. What unexpressable joy to have the greatest desire of her heart fulfilled by the mysterious hand of God!

But after many years of longing for this child, how could Hannah keep her promise to God? How could she leave her young son at the temple to serve the Lord under the guidance of Eli the priest?

Hannah was able to keep her vow because she trusted in the Lord. She knew Samuel was not hers alone. He belonged first and foremost to God, to the One who loved him with an infinite and perfect love. It was that knowledge which enabled her to love her long-awaited son with an open hand, allowing him to become all that God intended. Because Hannah could see beyond her own desires, beyond her own plans for her boy, he was able to grow up to become a prophet of the Lord. Because she could release him, it was he who played that crucial role in the history of the Hebrew people—anointing first Saul and then David as king over Israel.

PRAYER: Lord, please enable us to love with open hands these children which you have entrusted to our care. Let not our own selfish desires and finite plans limit their potential to fulfill the special purposes which You intend. Amen.

Lonely Cries

Song of Solomon 2:14.
>"My dove, hiding in the clefts of the rock,
>in the coverts of the cliff,
>show me your face,
>let me hear your voice;
>for your voice is sweet
>and your face is beautiful" *(Jerusalem Bible).*

*S*andy closed her magazine, turned out the living room light, and headed down the hall to her bedroom. As she passed Beth's doorway, she stopped briefly to check on her and then continued on her way into their cozy bedroom. On a cold winter's evening like this one, with Brian out of town on business, this was usually her favorite place to be. She would tuck herself in with the electric blanket turned up to "toast" and read a good book for company. But tonight she felt uneasy and found little comfort in the apartment without Brian.

Brian's job had always required him to travel. In the early years of their marriage Sandy had enjoyed both the freedom this allowed her to pursue outside interests and the time it had given her to spend with other friends.

But since Beth had become a part of their family, her feelings and situation had changed. Now it was important for Sandy to spend most of her evenings at home. Their tiny one needed the security of her parents, and since Brian had little choice about where he spent his own time, the responsibility of staying with

Beth had come to rest primarily on Sandy's shoulders. Even though she counted this both a joy and a privilege, the adjustment in her own lifestyle had been considerable.

This evening she missed Brian more than ever. It wasn't because she needed someone to help fill some empty hours. Quite the opposite!—it was because her life was fuller than ever, and now there was much more to share. Their daughter was entering an exciting stage of development; each day held new accomplishments and new expressions. And Sandy was learning much about herself that was exciting, challenging, and scary all at once. She wanted so much to share these discoveries with the person she loved most.

As she pulled the warm blanket even closer about her, she thought, *Who but Brian would be interested in something so personal?* It was then, in the midst of her loneliness, that God's Word began to play upon the edges of her mind. She felt her Father's heart calling to her own with love. He was reminding her that nothing was more important to him than the cry of his beloved child.

PRAYER: Thank you, Lord, for Your Spirit who seeks us out and reminds us that we are loved by You. Thank you that You desire to hear our every thought and in us You see such beauty. We often forget the depth of Your love and that we can turn to You at all times. Thank you that You are an intimate God, One who cares about every detail of our lives. Amen.

A Delightful Surprise

Psalm 107:8. Oh that men would praise the LORD for his goodness, and for his wonderful works to the children of men! (KJV).

That's funny. I could have sworn I left Christopher on his tummy, I thought as I passed by the cradle where he was now sleeping soundly—on his back. *Maybe I just forgot.* After all, I was busy trying to finish the housework before he woke from his mid-morning nap. The cradle was set up in a corner of the dining room so that I could keep an eye on him as I took care of my downstairs chores. As I gently rolled him over onto his stomach, I felt a tiny tug on my heartstrings when I realized how fast he was growing and that soon he would surely outgrow his cradle.

A little later, after moving the dining room chairs away from the table, I was running the vacuum over the rug when I just happened to glance up in Christopher's direction. There he was, in what looked like a very awkward position. With one arm thrown above his head he was pushing with all his strength, and I watched in amazement as he moved himself very slowly up, up, and finally onto his back.

I dropped my vacuum immediately and scooped my son up in my arms for a big bear hug. "Oh, Christopher, I'm so proud of you! That's quite an accomplishment you've made!" What a delightful surprise God placed in the midst of a very ordinary morning!

PRAYER: Dear Lord, we praise You for the joy we experience as we watch our children grow and develop. Their first major accomplishments bring smiles to the whole family. Oh, God, You are so good. Thank you for sprinkling these unexpected delights in the middle of very ordinary days–delights that strengthen us with Your joy. Amen.

Partnership That Reassures

Romans 8:28. We know that in everything God works for good with those who love him, who are called according to his purpose.

I find that since Christopher's birth I take life much more seriously. It's now difficult for me to turn on the television casually or thumb through a newspaper. The pain and destruction I read of in the headlines are deeply disturbing. And I grow angry with the many television programs that portray violent fantasies and degrading values.

I also catch myself worrying about many things that didn't concern me before. I knew evil existed in this world, but I did not fully understand its pervasiveness until I became responsible for such a vulnerable human being. Now I understand the temptation of becoming an overly protective parent. How can I help Christopher grow up to be a healthy, sensitive, loving man of God? When I listen to the media, I feel as though the odds are against me!

But the voice of the evil one is not the only voice to be heard in our world today. As I search the Scriptures, I discover how over and over again, just when it appears that Satan has the battle well in hand, God robs him of his victory. I see this occur in the cross, and I experience it in my own life as well.

Our Lord promises that even the negative influences and the destructive power at work in this world can be transformed, that by his power even they can work together for good for those who love him and are called according to his purpose.

I am thankful that God has the last word concerning the growth and maturation of our child. CT and I are not solely responsible but are partners with the all-powerful and all-knowing Lord of the universe.

PRAYER: Oh, Lord, thank you for the way You mysteriously hold the upper hand in our lives. Show us how to teach our children to love You. Give us wisdom as we help these wards search for Your purpose. Amen.

A Mothers' Sharing Group

Hebrews 10:24–25. Let us consider how to stir up one another to love and good works, not neglecting to meet together, as is the habit of some, but encouraging one another, and all the more as you see the Day drawing near.

*I*t had been a wonderful meeting. Ten of us, bound together by our common experience of being new mothers, gathered to study, share, and pray. This was a safe place, a refuge from the demands of our jobs and families. Here, once a week, we laughed and cried together, sharing our deepest joys and fears as each one in her own way sought to follow the Lord's path through the complicated maze of her daily life. No matter what failures or frustrations the week had held, we experienced the love and acceptance of the Lord through our sisters in Christ.

As I picked up stray cups, folded chairs, and cleaned out the coffee pot, I remembered how our meetings began. Christopher was just three months old. He was not a child who slept much; so most of my day was spent entertaining him. There was little time for study or conversation, and I felt exhausted, lonely, and bored. Before his birth I had been a career woman, and now the lack of mental challenge and the absence of co-workers to share with was difficult for me to adjust to. Although I felt God calling me to remain at home caring for my little boy, I was beginning to wonder if I could handle the loneliness.

My relationship with CT was beginning to feel the strain as well. Instead of expressing my loneliness, fear, and boredom, I criticized his lack of understanding. The more I criticized, the quieter he became and the lonelier I got.

Then, one day after church I mentioned my feelings of isolation to another mother in the nursery. She could identify with them immediately. It was as if a floodgate opened and we shared our common trials and joys. Time passed quickly, and soon both our husbands wandered into the nursery in search of their families.

In our last parish I had seen a mothers' sharing group operate, and from that chance meeting it seemed timely to start one here as well. As a result, we no longer bear our burdens alone. The Lord has used these women to encourage and minister to one another as we gather together in his love.

PRAYER: Thank you, Lord, for placing us in Your body, the church. Help us to reach out to one another when we feel trapped and alone. Amen.

Persevering and Trusting

Philippians 3:13–14. No, dear brothers, I am still not all I should be but I am bringing all my energies to bear on this one thing: Forgetting the past and looking forward to what lies ahead, I strain to reach the end of the race and receive the prize. . . . (*The Living Bible*).

*I*t had been five months since little Sarah's arrival, and Susan had been working diligently at her diet, suffering only a few minor setbacks when she attempted to eat away her "new baby blues." After putting Sarah down for her afternoon nap, Susan headed for the bedroom and her pre-pregnancy wardrobe. Surely there must be something there that would fit her by now!

She began with her favorite dress. As she pulled it out of the closet, she remembered the last time she had worn it. It had been their wedding anniversary, and she and her husband had spent a special evening together—sharing a meal at their favorite restaurant and later dancing well into the small hours of the morning. The silky feel of the fabric reminded her of how slim and pretty she had felt as they circled the dance floor.

But that had been a year and a half before, and her body had undergone a radical change since then. Her weight gain alone had been some forty pounds during her pregnancy. Yet now, just five months after having given birth, she had lost all but eight of them.

With much hope of receiving some sort of reward for good

behavior, she slipped the dress over her head. What a disappointment! In spite of all the weight she had lost, the buttons on the left side would not meet their mates on the right.

How tempting it was to give up at this point! The realization that her body would never again be quite the same fell upon her with new force. As if a veil had been removed, she saw with new clarity how the whole process of pregnancy and birth had caused her body to change, and her hips to round out much fuller than before.

It was in this moment of despondency that she turned, once again, to the Lord. Yes, she realized, she would have to continue her discipline of exercise and diet; but the rest she could leave to the Lord. She knew he would not abandon her but that even in this time of readjustment God would accomplish something new and wonderful. Perhaps, at some point in the future, she would find that her old figure had returned. Or perhaps the Lord had something else in store. Whatever the outcome, she knew in that moment of prayer that he wanted only the best of her. So she sought to trust in him.

PRAYER: Dear God, as we grow discouraged with ourselves, remind us that we are not solely dependent upon our own resources. Help us recommit ourselves to You so that we might receive Your help in time of need. Amen.

Teething: Another Hurdle

Romans 5:3–5. We also boast of our troubles, because we know that trouble produces endurance, endurance brings God's approval, and his approval creates hope. This hope does not disappoint us, for God has poured out his love into our hearts by means of the Holy Spirit, who is God's gift to us (TEV).

Just when I think our lives have finally settled down, Christopher encounters another hurdle. One of his lower incisors is ready to break through the skin, and it's driving both of us crazy!

He is the crankiest I have seen him in his young life. His nose is constantly running, and his eyes are red and teary. He won't eat, and his sleep is interrupted throughout the night with pitiful little cries. He doesn't want to be held, and he doesn't want to be left alone. Poor little guy, his gums must be at that awful painful-itchy stage. He is miserable, and I am sure that he doesn't understand why.

Christopher's irritableness is very wearing on mom as well. After listening to him fuss for hours on end, I begin to lose my perspective and become touchy and irritable myself. But that's not the most difficult thing for me to deal with. The part which is so disheartening is my feeling of helplessness. Everything I do to alleviate Christopher's discomfort proves fruitless. At this point the only avenue left open is simply to stay with my son and wait it out together.

Patience—that's one commodity I've always been short of. I'm a person of action, and waiting for things to run their course naturally has never been my forte! It looks as though God is going to allow Christopher's troubles to cultivate a little patience, endurance, and hope within me. It's just one of the fringe benefits of being a mom!

PRAYER: Dear Father, thank you for the assurance that You are at work within both us and our children during these trying times. Help us to be open to You in order that You might use these times to conform us more and more into the image of Your Son. Instill in us the patience to endure our families' hardships, deepen the love You've placed in our hearts, and grant us the hope that will lift our spirits. Amen.

Seeking Wisdom About Working

Psalm 32:8.

The LORD says, "I will teach you the way you should go; I will instruct you and advise you" (TEV).

*J*ill could feel the knots tightening in her stomach. It happened every time she attempted to wade through the stack of monthly bills.

She had left her job six months ago, just before Heather was born. When she first came home from the hospital with her tiny new charge, the excitement and experience of being a new mother overshadowed everything else. But as the months passed and her baby's needs grew, so did the family's financial burden. Every month they fell a little further behind, and they were beginning to feel the pinch of living on just one income.

Jill felt responsible for things being tight. After all, it was her paycheck that the family was missing. Even though her husband had been very much involved in making the decision that she would stay home with Heather, the financial stress was beginning to take its toll on their relationship. They were both more irritable than usual. Neither wanted to cast the blame for their increasingly restricted lifestyle on the other; yet both did so against their wills.

"Should I go back to work?" she wondered. "What about a part-time job? Maybe I could start my own business and work out of my home? If I did that, I would only have to leave Heather a minimal amount of time." She considered many options. She wanted to do what was best: best for Heather, best for her husband, and best for herself.

Jill knew that she needed to know the mind of Christ, for only with his wisdom could she make a decision that would result in the ultimate good for everyone. To do otherwise, to rely on human reason alone, would only mean continued subjection to the tunnel vision of anxiety and fear. It was time to turn to God.

PRAYER: Lord, we need to know Your will for our lives and for our families. We want to walk in faith with You, for we know that You will provide. Yet we don't want to be foolish—insisting that You work only one way, when You may well be opening another avenue of provision. Help us walk that fine line of obedience, the one that marks the edge of faith. Amen.

Sowing Seed in a Child's Life

Read Matthew 13:3–9, 18–23.

Matthew 13:8–9. "Other seeds fell on good soil and brought forth grain, some a hundredfold, some sixty, some thirty. He who has ears, let him hear."

A sower went out to sow. . . ." This must be one of the most familiar passages in Scripture. I've heard the story so many times that I can repeat it by heart. We can learn many lessons from this parable, most of which warn us about the condition and desires of our own hearts. But since I've become a parent, this parable has new meaning for me.

I can now place myself in the shoes of the sower instead of relating only to the conditions of the soil! What type of seed am I casting upon the developing person of my son? Am I sowing the seeds of the kingdom of God, or are the seeds of my own sin germinating in his soul instead?

One of a mother's greatest joys is to see her likeness reflected in her child. What a wonderful feeling when she finally sees that all the hours spent teaching and modeling the good and true things of life have taken root and are beginning to grow! But seeing her own image in the child can be a double-edged sword. What guilt and sadness accompany her awareness when her unintentional acts, her seemingly hidden feelings of anger and selfishness have borne their fruits as well!

What kind of sowing have I begun in my child's life? Christopher is still too young to see what type of plants will poke their heads through the soil of his personality. I know the weeds of sin will be present, for that's part of our human condition. But I can choose from which bag I draw my seed: that of my own selfishness and pride or that which glorifies God and promotes his presence in Christopher's life.

God presented me with a great challenge and responsibility when he entrusted Christopher to my care. May he also grant me the ability to be a wise sower of his word.

PRAYER: Dear Father, we pray that our children's souls will be fertile ground for the planting of Your word. Allow us the courage as parents to say no to the sin within ourselves and to plant only from the goodness and truth of Your kingdom. Amen.

Joy in a New Purpose

Psalm 4:8.
    You put gladness into my heart,
    more than when grain and wine abound (NAB).

CT and I sat sipping cool drinks as Christopher napped beside us in the shade of a colorful beach umbrella. A gentle offshore breeze took the unbearable edge off the afternoon heat. It was late summer, and we were enjoying a relaxing vacation on Cape Cod with CT's family.

As we listened to the rhythmic sound of waves breaking on the shore and watched gulls turn in the crystal blue sky, we reflected on all the changes we had experienced in just four short months. We had known that life would be different with a new baby in the family, but there was nothing, we agreed, that could have prepared us for how different things would be!

With a wide smile CT talked about the incredible joy he felt the first time Christopher looked up at him with recognition in his eyes. I shared the great pride that swells my heart when I take him to the grocery store and shoppers tell me what a beautiful son I have. Intermingled with our joys were words about the dirty diapers, the sleepless nights, and our diminished time for each other.

While sharing our thoughts, feelings, and experiences as new parents, I noticed a common thread weaving them all together. That thread was the joy we found in the new purpose God had placed in our lives when he gave Christopher to us. In that moment all the self-sacrifice seemed worthwhile. Caring for Christopher provided us with a purpose so satisfying and a task so rewarding that no other earthly treasure could deserve greater effort. By setting Christopher in our family, God had called us beyond our human capabilities—both in the giving of ourselves and in the receiving of his boundless joy.

PRAYER: Lord God, You grant us such a treasure when you give us children. The joy which they bring to us is immeasurable. And the blessings they share surpass anything else that is of this world. Thank you for bringing them into our lives. Amen.

Needing Our Helpmate's Help

Genesis 2:18. Then the LORD God said, "It is not good for the man to live alone. I will make a suitable companion to help him" (TEV).

When Dan arrived home from the office, the house was dark except for a single light upon the stairs. It had been a long day, and finding Anna sound asleep conjured up mixed emotions within him. On the one hand, he would have liked her company as he wound down from the frantic pace at work; on the other, he knew she needed some rest. Weighing the two options, he decided to enjoy a few moments alone.

As he reached for a box of crackers on the top shelf of the kitchen cupboard, he loosened his tie and unbuttoned the neck of his shirt. Then he made his way to his favorite chair in the living room, where he put his feet up on the coffee table and turned on a late-night news program. He needed some time to relax—a time when no one expected anything from him—so that the tightness in his chest might ease.

Lately, the stress had become unbearable. Just before Allyce was born, he had been promoted to the next level of management. At the time, he and Anna had celebrated this good fortune because they felt that with her income curtailed for a while, the extra money would be much needed. One thing they had not considered, however, was the effect that the added pressure at work combined with the addition of a new child at home would have upon their family.

He found life at home overwhelming. Before, home for him had always been a place of refuge from the pressures of his job. Now he encountered new demands there as well. He would arrive home only to find that Anna could hardly wait for his extra pair of hands to care for a screaming baby so that she could finish some other task. Now there was no time just to kick back and relax; and because of the pressure, he and Anna seemed to argue more than ever.

The most difficult thing for Dan to handle, however, was the lack of support he felt from his wife. Tonight was a perfect example. He was used to talking over his day with her and sharing his many trials, but now Anna didn't have the energy to wait up for him. He understood why but still missed their time together. He was beginning to feel like a stranger in his own home—watching a new relationship build between his wife and daughter at the very time when he felt distant from them.

The demands placed on every area of his life seemed to be pushing him to the breaking point. He was trying to please his boss, his wife, his child, and himself all at the same time. He was in a no-win situation, and he knew it!

Dan felt alone and overwhelmed. Something had to change. As he prayerfully weighed his options, he discovered that there were no easy answers. What he could do, however, was to share his struggles with Anna, in the hopes that together they might seek the Lord and his wise guidance. With that resolution, he rose from his chair, turned off the TV, and began climbing the stairs to share a midnight chat with his helpmate for life.

PRAYER: Lord God, how can we better support our spouses in the midst of all the new stresses and strains which we are under ourselves? Sometimes it seems as if life together is too much for both of us to bear. But You gave us to each other to be lifelong companions. Enable us to lift each other's spirits when we have no strength of our own to give. Help us to depend on You. Amen.

When "Squeaky Wheels" Make Our Decisions

Proverbs 3:6. In everything you do, put God first, and he will direct you and crown your efforts with success (*The Living Bible*)

O ur family operates on the "squeaky wheel" principle: the member or household item that makes the most noise is the one that receives the lion's share of attention.

These days, though, there are so many "squeaky wheels" in our house that it is hard to decide where to put my energy. Christopher has been the wheel which has received the most attention. Because he has been the top priority for many months, other wheels have gone out of alignment and need some fast attention.

One of those other wheels is my relationship with CT. Because we haven't had time just for us, our relationship is beginning to suffer from neglect. We are beginning to feel that we should try to put our jobs and Christopher's demands aside—if only for a moment—so that we can find some time to play together and nurture one another.

Another wheel is the time we have just for ourselves: time to read, pursue a hobby, or just relax. Our lives are so full right now that this kind of time has been crowded out by other urgent demands.

We are beginning to realize that the "squeaky wheel" method of decision making is not necessarily the best way to make our choices. We have found that noise does not always equal importance and that, when we let them, more subtle dimensions of our lives can slip away unnoticed. More and more we find ourselves reacting to situations instead of consciously planning our days.

One area in which this is especially true is in my time with the Lord. If I don't plan for some quiet moments with God, such moments just will not happen. The reason is simple—it's one relationship that doesn't scream for my attention. But I know that if I don't consistently invest my time there, all my other relationships are going to suffer.

Keeping God first in all we do—if CT and I can accomplish that, then surely the Lord will direct our decisions in all the other areas of our family life. Only then, only as we see with his eyes, will we be able to discern the truly important from mere noise and give even the "quiet" areas of our lives the attention they deserve.

PRAYER: Lord Jesus, forgive us when we neglect our relationships with You in order to take care of the "squeaky wheels" in our lives. You are so patient and understanding that we often forget that You are also a jealous God. Help us not to turn to You only when life becomes unbearable but in our daily lives as well. By Your Spirit enable us to open our hearts to You moment by moment so that Your subtle presence won't be crowded out. Amen.

Growing Up and Tasting Freedom

John 8:31–32. "If you continue in my word, you are truly my disciples, and you will know the truth, and the truth will make you free."

I have stopped thinking of Christopher's age in terms of weeks. This occurred to me when introducing him to a new friend today. "How old is the little guy?" the older gentleman asked with a smile. Instead of my usual reply of ten or fifteen or twenty weeks, I said, "Five months." This marks a change in my attitude. I'm beginning to let go and to acknowledge the fact that this tiny one is, indeed, growing up.

How exciting it is to be allowed the privilege of watching a child grow day by day! Sometimes their growth and development sneak up on you. Today I realized that by stating Christopher's age in terms of weeks, I was trying to keep him tiny and dependent as long as possible.

Now that I see him as five months old, I realize in a new way that he is no longer that passive baby we brought home from the hospital. He can place objects in his mouth and entertain himself. He has experienced the power of filling a room with the sound of his own voice. And he is strong enough to hold his head up, look around, and begin to satisfy his own curiosity.

God's intention for us is that we be free—free to become the persons that we were intended to be. It hadn't occurred to me, however, that Christopher would begin to experience a taste of that wonderful freedom this early in his life.

PRAYER: Lord, open our eyes that we might see Your subtle hand at work molding and shaping the development of our children. Grant us the wisdom to know how to encourage them with every new step of growth. Amen.

One Woman's Secret

Read Proverbs 31:10–31.

Proverbs 31:10–11. How hard it is to find a capable wife! She is worth far more than jewels. Her husband puts his confidence in her, and he will never be poor (TEV).

I have always struggled with Ruby. That's the name I've given to the role model of a perfect wife found in this passage from Proverbs. She has posed a challenge, a burden, and sometimes even a threat to me. I've often thought that the person describing this ideal wife must have been a man, for any honest woman would know in her heart that it's just not possible to be all things to all people. Since I've become a mother, however, the spirit of this passage has spurred me on to search for that key which could unlock the potential to become my very best.

According to Proverbs, an accomplished wife is a woman who remains true to who she is through all the phases and stages of life. She lives life to the fullest and utilizes all her talents to the best of her ability. She is not afraid to take on any God-given challenge that presents itself. She keeps her home in order and her family well provided for. She is a profit-making businesswoman who knows the value of what she has to offer. She is strong and generous, and the words she speaks are those of kindness and wisdom. Finally, she is loved by her family, and she fills her husband with pride.

Whew! How could anyone measure up to that? What was Ruby's secret? How could she wear all those hats and not grow weary? Some days I can barely deal with my job, let alone the needy family I find when I come through the kitchen door. As a businesswoman, she must have suffered the same stress working mothers do today. How is it that her children didn't resent the time she spent at work or that her husband didn't become jealous of her success? Where did she find her strength?

What is a woman's secret for strength, courage, and creativity? Scripture tells us—through the ideal presented by Ruby—that it is the fear of the Lord. Through her *faith* in God Ruby found the courage to become all she was meant to be and found the wisdom and humility to do so in such a way as to remain a blessing to all those around her.

PRAYER: Dear Lord, in those times when we want to run from You in the midst of all the stress and confusion that the daily demands of family and work place upon us, give us the courage and strength to continue to strive for only Your best. Grant us the wisdom to distinguish between those tasks You would have us do and those meant for other hands, so that we, like Ruby, might hit our best stride for a lifetime of serving You. Amen.

The Best I Have to Offer

Genesis 18:1-3, 8. As Abraham was sitting at the entrance of his tent during the hottest part of the day, he looked up and saw three men standing there. "Sirs, please do not pass by my home without stopping; I am here to serve you." He took some cream, some milk, and the meat, and set the food before the men (TEV).

CT and I love to entertain. We enjoy setting a fine table with our best china and table linens and sharing our favorite foods with friends. Many of our best memories are of times spent after dinner lingering over coffee around the dining room table in heartfelt conversation with friends and family. In our house food always seems to be the key which opens the door to good discussion.

How quickly all of that has changed! Now, where flowers and candlesticks used to sit you'll find a table covered with diapers, baby clothes, and blankets. The dining room has become a "baby's rest area!" On one side of the hutch sits a changing table, while on the other stands a cradle. And scattered around the floor are toys and other miscellaneous items brought downstairs to save me from unneccesary trips to the second floor. The prospect that our new baby would literally take over our home hadn't occurred to me!

For the first few months of Christopher's life, the thought of receiving unexpected company was cause for great panic! Like Abraham and Sarah, I wanted to offer my guests our best. For me, at the very least, that meant a neat and tidy home. So the clutter was cause for much embarrassment, and the joy I once found in entertaining guests seemed lost.

I started paying attention to the way my husband and visitors reacted to our home. CT didn't mind the disorder. He was so proud of his new son that he was happy to show him off to anyone who happened to come to our door. Our friends weren't put off by the disarray, either. They didn't expect an orderly house. Besides, they had come to see us and were happy to accept us just the way they found us. It seemed I was the only one who appeared bothered by the mess.

God has taught me another lesson of love. The very best that I have to offer to those around me is not necessarily the food I prepare or the house I present. It is not the things I do but, rather, most importantly, it is the person that I am.

PRAYER: Dear God, help us to relax and enjoy the relationships that You have put into our lives. In the midst of the chaos which occurs when we bring a new baby home, grant us the grace to offer what we have and to accept that which is beyond our ability to give. Amen.

Finding the Present's Joy

Ecclesiastes 3:1. To every thing there is a season, and a time to every purpose under the heaven (KJV).

---

*P*aula stood at the end of the driveway, adjusting Rebecca's position in the baby carrier as they waited for her mother to join them for an early morning walk. The morning was brisk, and the rich scent of northwestern pines hung in the air. As Paula's mother approached, Paula fell into step.

It had become their habit to walk together several times a week during Paula's pregnancy. Now they kept their appointments because they had come to enjoy both the exercise and each other's company. This was their time to catch up with each other. The shared experience of motherhood had brought a new closeness to their relationship.

Paula found that she did most of the talking, probably because her life had seen such radical change and there was so much "newness" confronting her. She was looking forward to regaining more control over her life. As a result, many of her statements began with the phrase "I can hardly wait until. . . ." From there a variety of endings could be interchanged: "Rebecca can feed herself so I can enjoy a meal"; "Rebecca can entertain herself so I can get some housework done"; or "Rebecca starts nursery school so I can have some time to myself."

Paula's mother recognized her daughter's tendency to look ahead, and she knew it was because Paula hoped the future would be better than the present—that the satisfaction would be greater or the purposes higher. It was a tendency that she had experienced in the different seasons of her own life, and only recently had she come to realize how looking forward to spring can rob winter of much of its joy.

As gently as she could, Paula's mother shared her own experience. She talked of the joy that she had *learned* to find in the present and how much richness this new perspective had added. It didn't mean giving up the hope which the future holds. It meant to embrace, in addition, the wondrous ways in which God was acting even now.

PRAYER: Thank you, Lord, for the hope which the future holds, but also and most especially, for the many joys to be found in the present. Open our eyes that we might see those joys and experience them to the fullest. Help us to be wholly present to the season of life which we are in. Amen.

Placing Our Children in the Lord's Hands

Matthew 19:14–15. But Jesus said, "Let the little children come to me, and don't prevent them. For of such is the Kingdom of Heaven." And he put his hands on their heads and blessed them before he left (*The Living Bible*).

*L*ord Jesus, please bless and keep Christopher. Grace him with a peaceful night's sleep. Set Your angels guard over him, protecting him from all evil. Allow Your Spirit to guard his thoughts and inspire his dreams, that he might be enabled to grow up to be a true man of God and accomplish all the purposes which You intend for him. May he become closer to You, Lord, with every breath he takes. And may Your peace, love, and joy rest upon him always. Amen." As CT and I finished our evening prayers with Christopher, we tucked him snugly into his crib. This is the way we end our days now, with these very special moments together as a family before the Lord.

This is our way of bringing Christopher to Jesus, that he might be touched and blessed and claimed by God. We simply place him in Jesus' hands. He is too small to voice any objections. I know that taking Christopher to Jesus the way we do now is much easier than it will be to allow him to go to the Master on his own in the future.

In what ways might we hamper our son in his relationship with God? Will we push Christopher at Christ because our faith is very important to us? Will we assume a relationship that isn't there or isn't as personally developed as we would expect? Because our feelings on the subject are quite strong, will we squelch any questions and doubts that he might have? Or will we hamper Christopher's access to Jesus by limiting his experience and perceptions to that of our own?

My desire for Christopher is that his faith might grow deeper and stronger through the years naturally. I want to provide the right kind of help along the way. May the Lord grant me sensitivity both to his Spirit and my son's.

PRAYER: Here we go again, Lord, wondering about the future! Our concern stems from our love for our children and a desire to do our best as parents. Free us from our fears, Lord, and inform us as to how we can allow our children to come to You. Help us to act appropriately in the different situations which will occur at each season of our family's lives. Amen.

Needing a Greater Challenge

Proverbs 31:10-11, 16, 18.

> A good wife who can find?
> She is far more precious than jewels.
> The heart of her husband trusts in her,
> and he will have no lack of gain.
> She considers a field and buys it;
> with the fruit of her hands she plants a
> vineyard.
> She perceives that her merchandise is
> profitable.
> Her lamp does not go out at night.

*S*heryl was finally going back to work. On Monday she would return to the hospital to continue pursuing the medical career she loved and had worked hard to prepare for. *It will feel so good to be back in the lab,* she thought.

Sheryl's six-month maternity leave had been a real struggle. She loved Eliza, her newborn daughter, but didn't feel quite at ease staying home all day. As the days passed, she became more and more restless. She missed the regular routine her job provided and the challenge each day at the hospital brought. She had been one of the top people in her lab. She was good at problem solving and being involved with medicine that often meant she played a key role in restoring a person's health. She liked feeling that all her skills and knowledge were being pushed to the limit and that what she did made a real difference in the lives of others.

During her maternity leave, on the other hand, some of the greatest challenges she met—after providing for her daughter's basic needs—were discovering the cheapest place to buy disposable diapers and which grocery store carried the right brand of formula. She was growing bored and felt boredom creeping into her marriage. "How can I be a good wife and mother when I'm so unhappy with myself?" she wondered. As her anxiety built, so did her baby's. It was at this point, when she was feeling restless with herself and afraid that that restlessness was being communicated to Eliza, that her decision was made. She would return to work as soon as her maternity leave had ended.

PRAYER: Dear Lord, we, like the person in Proverbs, are women of many gifts and talents. And we are blessed that You, our Creator, did not cut us all out of the same dough with the same old cookie cutter. You make each one of us unique, with a special purpose all our own. Then you relate to us as individuals, pointing out a path that suits both us and our life situations. Lord Jesus, help us each to be true to the person You created, for then we will be the best parents and spouses possible. Amen.

A Father's Growing Pleasure

Hebrews 11:1. Now faith is the assurance of things hoped for, the conviction of things not seen.

Jeff towered over his daughter as she sat smiling up at him from her infant seat on the kitchen floor. He was on his way to work, and as he put his coat on, her crooked smile caught his eye. Although he was running late, he couldn't resist taking a moment to crouch down and tickle little Emily's ribs and join her in her infectious laughter. Then he grabbed his keys, flew out the door, and was off for another day of work.

"It's finally beginning to happen," Bev sighed to herself as she witnessed this scene from the kitchen doorway. Jeff was not one of those fathers who cooed and cuddled with their newborn. In fact, the only times Bev had seen him hold Emily were those when she had emphatically placed her into his awkward arms. Emily's twenty-some-odd inches appeared to make him aware of every bit of his six feet of height. He looked about as comfortable with Emily in his rough hands as he did holding a delicate piece of porcelain.

Once, Jeff had confessed that it was hard to feel a real connection with his daughter, especially when all she seemed to do was eat, sleep, and spit up! He felt that he had very little to offer at this stage in her life and that it was Mommy who appeared to have it all.

But while Jeff was not a terribly demonstrative man, Bev knew that he felt his love deeply. She had experienced it herself in many subtle ways throughout their own relationshp. So she had faith that his love for Emily would surface as well and that he would come to express it more easily as Emily's own awareness and responsiveness grew.

Now, as she watched the scene in the kitchen and listened to their laughter, Bev saw God fulfilling her hopes and answering her prayers. Jeff was reaching out to his little girl and beginning to enjoy her presence within their family. Bev then knew that as Emily grew, so would her experience of her daddy's love.

PRAYER: Lord Jesus, help us to trust You as You work in our husbands' lives. Often it is difficult for us to discern their true feelings. Give us patience, Lord, that we might allow them to share their emotions in Your time. Help us to have faith that You will enable them to reach out with the father-love which You have planted deep within and share that love with their children. Amen.

Opening Ourselves to Life

Matthew 18:2–4. So Jesus called a child, had him stand in front of them, and said, "I assure you that unless you change and become like children, you will never enter the Kingdom of heaven. The greatest in the Kingdom of heaven is the one who humbles himself and becomes like this child" (TEV).

---

*T*hat's quite some balancing act!" I laughed as I watched Christopher sitting tenuously on a quilt in the middle of the living room floor. I don't know how such a little body can hold up that huge head! Oops! There he goes. He's down again after a valiant attempt to hold himself in an upright position.

I'm having so much fun watching my son grow. Each new expression, every awkward attempt at some sort of mobility is a thrill to behold. He brings a fresh perspective to every new encounter. Each day holds new discoveries—as his awareness expands, so does his world. And I get to rediscover the world with him!

Approaching each new day with a fresh perspective—that must be part of what Jesus meant when he said that we are to become like little children. Often I miss much of what God would teach me because I assume I already know what he has to say, or I've already been through a situation before. But God often uses similar situations to unveil different truths.

Walking through life with Christopher has brought new meaning to this passage from Matthew's Gospel for me. He is open to life and very able to encounter it freshly with each new day. Through his example I feel Christ calling me to hold myself open to life as well. I must believe that the Holy Spirit presents new opportunities for discovery each day and that to expect the unexpected is part of God's plan. I am to approach life with the eyes of a child.

PRAYER: Dear Lord, sometimes we forget that we don't know quite as much as we think we do, which limits the blessings which You can share with us. Teach us how to accept each day as if it was handed to us directly from You. Help us to approach life with childlike faith. Amen.

The Experience of Renewed Strength

Psalm 103:1–5.

Bless the LORD, my soul;
    my innermost heart, bless his holy name.
Bless the LORD, my soul,
    and forget none of his benefits.
He pardons all my guilt
    and heals all my suffering.
He rescues me from the pit of death
    and surrounds me with constant love,
        with tender affection;
he contents me with all good in the prime of life,
    and my youth is ever new like an eagle's (NEB).

What a glorious morning! my mind sang as I opened my eyes to a brilliant November day. From the warmth of my bed I could see that the trees outside my window had been brushed with the most delicate of late autumn frosts. I began to plan my day and to think about a walk outside where I could feel the crunch of the crisp frost underfoot. Later, I decided, I would bundle Christopher up in his snowsuit and put him in his stroller for a long walk. But for now, I was just going to enjoy this peaceful moment. It was a rare morning when both of my men were asleep at the same time.

I felt terrific! It was surprising to discover what a full night's sleep could do to replenish my strength—and it had been over a week since Christopher had awakened me during the dark morning hours.

I felt good in my body, and in my soul as well. While lying there in the morning sun, motherhood no longer seemed quite so overwhelming. Christopher and I appeared to have finally matched our strides—for the moment at least.

As I took a good long stretch, I thought about my experience of the first six months of parenthood. It seemed a little like what I imagined boot camp to be! I had been forced to confront many major issues in a relatively short period of time. Now, I hoped, the pace of this confrontation would slow down.

Having survived "parental boot camp," with God's help, I felt stronger and tougher than ever before. I felt that in helping me walk through the many trials, joys, and fears of the past six months, the Lord had strengthened me deep within.

God is so good, I thought. *He has showered his blessings upon me in uncounted ways. In the times when I was aware of my own shortcomings and sin, he touched me with his grace and assured me that by his Spirit he would enable me to raise Christopher as I ought. In times of sorrow and fear he lifted my heart by the presence of his constant love. And when I least expected it but needed it the most, he granted me that joy which surprises!*

Cuddled up under my warm blankets in that sun-filled room, I was filled with a sense of gratitude. God *had* renewed the strength within me! Though many trials no doubt still lay ahead, I knew then that he would continue to be with me. I knew that he would be "a lamp unto our feet" as my family moved on.

PRAYER: Lord Jesus, You are so good to us! You share with us the opportunity to raise Your children, and through the challenge of that experience You make us better people. In the years ahead, help us always to turn to You in the midst of both joy and trial. Remind us that in all things Your love will reign supreme when we turn to You in faith. Amen.